Preaching as
Local Theology
and Folk Art

Preaching as Local Theology and Folk Art

Leonora Tubbs Tisdale

Fortress Press
Minneapolis

PREACHING AS LOCAL THEOLOGY AND FOLK ART

Scripture quotations are from the New Revised Standard Version Bible, copyright © 1989 by the Division of Christian Education of the National Council of the Churches of Christ in the United States of America. Used with permission.

Interior design: Joseph Bonyata/David Lott
Cover design: Joseph Bonyata/David Lott
Cover art: Panels from Black Family Album quilt by Sara Ann Wilson, New Jersey or New York, 1854.

ISBN 0-8006-2773-3

The paper used in this book meets the minimum requirements of American National Standard for Information Sciences—Permanence of Paper for Printed Library Materials, ANSI Z329.48-1984.

Manufactured in the United States of America   AF 1-2773

8   9   10

For Alfred

Beloved partner
in the joyous dance
of life, love, and ministry

Contents

Acknowledgments

Books, like sermons, are not born in isolation, but in community. I have been aware, in the writing of this one, of the many saints who have helped to guide, encourage, correct, and sustain me in the process. For these especially, I am grateful:

• For Thomas G. Long, teacher, friend, and colleague—who helped me refine many of the ideas in this book while advising my doctoral dissertation, and whose support and encouragement have always made me want to become my best homiletical self.

• For Bernard Boyd (University of North Carolina–Chapel Hill) and F. Wellford Hobbie (Union Theological Seminary in Virginia), beloved professors who, though now deceased, live on in my memory as liberating teachers. The first encouraged me to read the Bible with my mind as well as my heart. The second encouraged me to preach the gospel.

• For the four congregations of the former Episcopal-Presbyterian Shared Ministry in central Virginia, who taught me to ask the right questions and who patiently trained me in the ways of contextual ministry.

• For seminary students and local pastors, who have willingly shared with me their own contextual stories and sermons and who, in the process, have taught me much.

• For Princeton Theological Seminary, which generously granted me an early sabbatical so that I could write this book.

• For David Bartlett, Fred Craddock, Janet Weathers, James F. Kay, Linda McKinnish Bridges, Rick Osmer, Carol Lakey Hess, Thomas Troeger, and Nancy Lammers Gross—valued colleagues who have also been cheerleaders and loving critics along the way.

• For my editor Cynthia Thompson, who has been an encourager as well as a wise and knowledgeable guide.

• For graduate student assistants Dana Wright and Kristin Saldine, who, respectively, prepared the bibliography and index, and helped with the proofreading.

• For the women of prayer groups in Richmond and Princeton—Kerry, Linda, Rosalind, Jean, Cathy, Karla, Carol, and Janet—sisters of Spirit and spunk.

• For my parents, Jim and Lee Tubbs—who have modeled for me, through their preaching and teaching, passionate and incarnate proclamation of the gospel, and who have supported me through their prayers, their love, and their physical presence in times of need.

• For my children, Leonora and William—wise, wonderful, and faith-full teenagers, who not only have been invested in this project from a very early age, but who also rank among the finest sermon critics I know.

• And for Al, my beloved husband—whose love and laughter have sustained me, whose faith and compassion have inspired me, and whose ministry models the folk dance I describe. It is to him this book is dedicated with love and deep gratitude for the many sacrifices he has made along the way.

Preface

Good preaching not only requires its practitioners to become skilled biblical exegetes. It also requires them to become adept in "exegeting" local congregations and their contexts, so that they can proclaim the gospel in relevant and transformative ways for particular communities of faith.

Unfortunately, however, homiletical texts and courses have not always attended as carefully or thoughtfully to the exegesis of contexts as they have to the exegesis of texts. While preachers have been provided with detailed methods for biblical interpretation, congregational interpretation has frequently been left to the intuition and hunches of the local pastor.

This book seeks to correct that imbalance. Operating on the assumption that there are a number of pastors and chaplains who, like cross-cultural missionaries, are actually proclaiming the gospel "across subcultures" (that is, preaching to people whose worldview and values are different from their own), this book addresses two questions:

First, How can preachers become better exegetes of local congregations and their subcultures?

And second, What difference does such knowledge make for local preaching—both in its theology and in its art (language, illustrations, and form)?

My own interest in these questions first arose while I was serving as pastor of four small "town and country" churches in central Virginia. Finding myself in the throes of culture shock, I struggled with how to proclaim the gospel in a more meaningful and relevant way to congregations whose assumptions not only differed from my own, but also differed from one another. Although I sometimes sensed that my sermons were "missing" my people, I did not always know how to preach in a way that was more fitting and appropriate for them.

Chapter 1 begins with a recounting of that experience and with a recognition that there are actually many pastors in the United States who, like cross-cultural missionaries, are struggling to proclaim the Gospel to people whose worlds are different from their own. Whether it be the "cosmopolitan" urban pastor who has recently been called to minister to a congregation of blue collar "locals," the Korean-American pastor whose congregation includes several diverse generations, the pastor of a rural congregation who also leads occasional worship services in a nearby prison, or the young chaplain struggling to prepare meaningful sermons for retirement home residents—preaching frequently requires its practitioners to proclaim the gospel across cultures. Consequently, pastors cannot readily assume that the assumptions they take into the pulpit, the illustrations they find most meaningful, or the sermon forms they most enjoy using will be equally accessible to or meaningful for their hearers. Indeed, they may well find that a gap exists between the pulpit and the pew—a gap they need help understanding and bridging.

In chapter 2 I propose that one way to bridge this gap is to view preaching as an act of constructing "local theology"—that is, theology crafted for a very particular people in a particular time and place. Like theologies that have emerged from base communities in Latin America, preaching is a highly contextual act, requiring its practitioners to consider context as seriously as they consider biblical text in the interpretive process. Indeed, if we preachers want to reflect in our own proclamation the God who became incarnate for our sakes (meeting us on our turf), to remove from our own preaching any "false stumbling blocks" that might hinder a faithful hearing of the gospel, and to bring the gospel and contemporary life together in ways that capture and transform congregational imaginations, then we necessarily must first attend carefully to the contexts in which we are preaching.

Consequently, in chapter 3 I turn toward the task of congregational exegesis, outlining a very practical method for interpreting congregational subcultures that can be engaged by busy pastors while carrying on the ordinary tasks of ministry. Drawing on the expertise of authors in the fields of congregational studies and cultural anthropology, this chapter identifies seven symbols of congregational life that hold particular promise for revealing cultural and theological identity, and provides interpretive frameworks through which the local pastor can deepen his or her understanding of the congregation's own worldview, values, and ethos. At stake is not only enhanced cultural understanding, but also a deepening awareness of the local theologies that already exist within the life of a congregation (beliefs regarding God, humanity, nature, time, the church, and their interrelationships).

Chapter 4 then turns to the question: "So, what difference does all this make for the theology of preaching?" Here we revisit the "text-to-sermon" process (revisioned as a "con/text-to-sermon" process), observing how greater attention to congregational context at each juncture—from the selection of biblical texts for proclamation, to the pastor's initial reading of them, to the methods used for biblical interpretation, to the discernment of fitting themes and strategies for proclamation—can positively contribute toward preaching as local theology. Sermons of local pastors, preached in their own unique congregational contexts, provide real-life examples of contextual theologizing in action.

Finally, in chapter 5, we turn toward the art of the sermon, exploring ways in which an enhanced emphasis upon contextuality in preaching can also contribute to sermons that are more fitting for local congregations in regard to their language, illustrations, and form. Here preaching is likened to folk art—more particularly to a circular folk dance—in which the preacher stays close to the ground of the hearers, enfleshing the sermon in language, rhythms, and forms that encourage local hearers to want to put on their own dancing shoes and join in the dance of faith.

In writing this book I have been aware of ways in which my own cultural contexts (past and present) have contributed to its perspectives. I am an Anglo-Saxon Protestant (Presbyterian) woman, who has lived most of her life in the Eastern part of the United States. Consequently, many of the stories I tell, examples and illustrations I use, and questions I address are reflective of those contexts and their congregations.

I have also been gifted with a number of international, ecumenical, and cross-cultural experiences in my ministry, however: serving as a volunteer missionary in South Korea, representing my denomination on the Central Committee of the World Council of Churches, pastoring both Episcopal and Presbyterian congregations, and teaching students of diverse cultures in several different seminaries. These experiences have deepened my questions, expanded my realm of conversation partners, and heightened my interest in cross-cultural issues. In many ways this book is my attempt to bring what I have learned about contextuality in more global forums to bear upon the particular and local instance of preaching in U. S. congregations.

As I have written, I also have tried to envision my own reading audience. Certainly local pastors, chaplains, and seminarians have been among those for whom I have hoped this book might prove beneficial. I also believe, however, that skills in congregational exegesis and contextual theologizing are equally critical for other areas of ministry. Thus I am hopeful that portions of this book might also prove useful for Christian educators, pastoral caregivers, and others charged with the spiritual and theological leadership of congregations.

Nora Tubbs Tisdale
Princeton Theological Seminary
Princeton, New Jersey

1
The Culture Shock of Preaching

In the late 1970s my husband Al and I spent a one-year seminary internship in South Korea, serving as volunteer missionaries of our denomination. Our assignment was to teach English conversation and theology in English at a theological seminary in Seoul.

During our year in Korea, we underwent considerable culture shock. The language was different; the food was different; the customs were different; the humor was different; the arts were different; and the church—its theology, ethos, and ritual life—was different from that to which we had become accustomed as white North American Protestants.

Fortunately, however, our denomination had done a good job of preparing us for the culture shock we would inevitably encounter. During the summer before our departure for Seoul, we gathered with other new missionaries at a denominational retreat center and heard lectures and presentations that acquainted us with the challenges of living in a foreign culture. Several Korean nationals and missionaries met with us, giving us an initial introduction to the history, geography, politics, and the philosophical and religious climate of the land to which we were headed. We read books about Korea, learned a bit of the language, and received instruction regarding the teaching of English as a second language. Theologians explored with us issues related to cross-cultural missions and indigenous theologies.

While no amount of prior training can ever totally ameliorate the shock that comes from immersion in a foreign culture, we found that our transition into Korean life was greatly eased by the careful preparation our denomination had given us. Perhaps most importantly, we approached matters of "difference" with greater empathy (and less frustration) because we had already been given a rudimentary understanding of some of the cultural underpinnings sustaining those differences.

When we returned to the United States, we completed our final year of seminary education, and ventured forth to try our wings in parish ministry. We were a strange breed in those days—a budding clergy couple in a denomination that had not yet seen many of our kind—and were delighted when four small "town and country" churches in central Virginia called us to be their pastors. We approached our new ministerial tasks with enthusiasm and excitement.

Before long, however, I began to realize that I was in the throes of "culture shock"—much like that which I had experienced as a missionary in Korea. Despite the fact that the people in these churches looked like me (white North American Protestants), talked like me (even to the extent of speaking a "Southern" brand of English), and were, in three of the four congregations, members of the same denomination, there were considerable cultural differences that existed between me and my parishioners. Only this time, no one had even warned me that I would encounter "culture shock"—much less prepared me for dealing with it.

The parish was an ecumenical one: three of the congregations were Presbyterian; one was Episcopal. Geographically, two of the churches (one Presbyterian and one Episcopal) were located in the small town where my husband and I lived. A third was twenty-five miles south of town in a rural area that was rapidly becoming a bedroom community for the state capital. The fourth was thirteen miles north of town, nestled in the midst of dairy farms.

My husband, who had grown up on a farm in a very small town, seemed to adjust more quickly and easily to our new environment than I. It did not take him long to feel "at home" there. But I—who had spent my entire life in large towns and cities and had spent most of my church life in congregations with over six hundred members—bore the brunt of congregational culture shock.

I still remember my first Sunday in my new parish. My official duties began at 10 A.M., as I led worship at one of the town churches. Then I travelled out into the country for my second service.

There were thirteen people in my second worshiping congregation that Sunday morning, and twelve of them sat in the back two rows of the church. The only one who sat up front near me was the organist. Between me and most of the congregation existed an enormous physical gulf. Admittedly, a lot of that gulf was due to the fact that I was the first woman this congregation had ever had as pastor, and the people were uncertain as to how this new arrangement was going to work. They were somewhat wary—adopting a "wait and see" attitude until they had assurance that I could indeed be an effective pastor in their midst.

But over time I also began to suspect that the physical gulf that existed between me and my worshiping congregation that first Sunday morning was symbolic of other differences that existed between us as well. For the truth was, we were—pastor and people—from very different worlds. And one of the places where our differences first became manifest for me was in the pulpit.

Culture Shock in the Parish Pulpit

The arrangement in this parish was that my husband and I each led worship in the same two congregations the first three Sundays of the month and swapped pulpits on fourth and fifth Sundays. The net result was that for five years we both preached—at least once a month—in all four of the churches.

I had not been pastor in this setting very long at all before I began experiencing frustration in my attempts to proclaim the gospel. Although I couldn't always name the problem, I sensed almost immediately that my preaching was not connecting with my new congregations as well as it might. On some Sundays, I felt that my sermons were "missing" them altogether.

For example, I realized (almost from the start) that if I made use of illustrative materials I had been encouraged to use while in seminary—such as vignettes from contemporary novels or plays—the effects were not always as I desired. Often the world portrayed in the latest Broadway play or in a contemporary novel seemed "citified" and far removed from my small congregations and their worlds. My parishioners, by and large, did not readily identify with questions raised by characters in a contemporary novel or with the view of the world assumed in a current play. Their world and their issues were different.

I also began puzzling over sermon "logic" and "affect." In seminary we had spent a great deal of time working on the logic of preaching; getting our sermons to flow with unity and coherence and clarity of purpose was a primary goal. From time to time, I liked to preach on the great doctrines of the church, explaining in a very rational way their meaning and import for our lives as Christians. Yet while several members of the town congregations always commented favorably on those sermons, my sense was that for some of my adult parishioners (especially those who had a high school education or less), sermons that employed abstract thought forms or that were structured according to an academic-style argument held little meaning or value. Almost by instinct I began to incorporate more narrative in my preaching, in part because storytelling seemed to be the one communicational mode I could depend upon to cross lines of education and age.

In terms of sermon "affect," I also experienced culture shock. During my first year in this parish I remember commenting (in great frustration) to my husband, "What these people want above all is preaching that *moves* them—that speaks to them on a deep and personal level about matters of faith and life—and I'm not even sure I *know* how to preach that way." What had "moved" a classroom of my peers in a seminary academic setting seemed to be very different from what "moved" a congregation comprised primarily of blue collar workers or of dairy farmers.

The differences that I perceived *between* me and my people were not the only factors that frustrated the preaching task in this multichurch parish, however; equally challenging were the differences that existed *among* those four churches that appeared, on the surface, to be very similar. Pastoring four churches was much like having four children—each with its own distinctive personality, character, and idiosyncrasies. Consequently, it was not uncommon for the same sermon—preached in four different settings—to elicit four totally different responses from the congregations. Indeed, there were many Sundays when I would take the very same sermon and preach it (with equal passion and enthusiasm) in two congregations—only to have it "fly" in one setting and "flop" in the other. I knew that the mysterious workings of the Holy Spirit had something to do with this phenomenon. I began to wonder, however, if other factors were also at work. What was it about a sermon that caused it to connect more effectively with one congregation than with another? What was it about a congregation that caused it to respond more favorably to one sermon than to another?

Culture Shock in the Prison Pulpit

In the meantime, my husband Al and some of our parishioners began leading a monthly worship service on Sunday evenings in a nearby state correctional institution for men. While Al had not encountered culture shock to the same degree that I had in those town and country churches, he did confront it in the prison. I used to await with great anticipation his arrival home late Sunday evening, so that I could hear him recount his own latest episode in cross-cultural preaching and worship.

The congregation that gathered for worship at our local correctional center for men typically numbered between fifteen and twenty; two-thirds were African American, one-third were Euro-American. The men had been incarcerated for various felonies and misdemeanors, and tended to stay in this particular correctional institution an average of two years. Many who attended the Sunday evening services had been churchgoers before they were confined, so they had some history and background in the Christian faith. Others had no previous church experience, but attended in order to gain a brief respite from the boredom of "lock-up." All were people who, because of their life circumstances, had little patience with platitudes or with trite answers to tough questions. They wanted to get to the heart of issues quickly and succinctly, and they demanded that preaching do the same.

Consequently the worship "ethos" in the prison was very different from that in any of our four congregations. The prisoners felt free to interrupt Al at random as he preached—either to ask a question (which might or might not have any relevance to the text and message he was preaching), to debate or affirm a point, or to pronounce (usually through a highly expressive expletive) that a particular point was untrue or irrelevant to their lives.

While Al frequently used the same biblical text(s) as the basis for his Sunday morning and Sunday evening proclamation, the similarity in sermons usually ended there. The radical shift in congregational worlds necessitated equally radical changes in preaching. My husband struggled to shape sermons that spoke simply, directly, and meaningfully to the needs of the prisoners. His Sunday evening sermons were generally shorter, had different examples, and were more dialogical in style than the ones preached on Sunday morning. The longer he led worship in the prison, the more "at home" he became in this strange, new world. And he always found worship with these fellow Christians to be deeply moving and meaningful.

But at first, the culture shock was acute. Despite Al's best homiletical efforts he frequently reported that the most meaningful part of the service—especially for those who had roots in the Christian faith—was not the sermon. Rather, what these men most valued was the group singing (especially of old-time gospel favorites) and the opportunity to pray aloud their own heartfelt confessions of sin.

Culture Shock among New Pastors

The culture shock Al and I experienced in our first parish is not, I am convinced, an uncommon occurrence for U.S. pastors. Profiles of seminarians indicate that the majority of them come to seminary from large congregations in urban or suburban settings,[1] but leave seminary to become pastors in far more diverse contexts. Some find themselves proclaiming the gospel in the "foreign" land of the inner city; others relocate to geographical regions of the United States whose customs and ways seem alien to them. Some undertake ministries that actually cross national, racial, or ethnic lines, while others follow the path of chaplaincy (ministering to communities comprised of college students, hospital or nursing home residents, military families, or prisoners). Many new pastors begin their parish ministry in settings akin to that in which my husband and I began ours—serving as pastors of the small town and country churches that comprise the vast majority of mainline congregations.

Whatever the setting for ministry, the fledgling pastor can undergo culture shock when the lifestyle, customs, and assumptions of those to whom she or he ministers differ significantly from the pastor's own. Bob, a pastor of six months in upstate New York who had completed a career in military service before entering seminary, approached me at a continuing education event to share his own frustrations as a preacher. "I left seminary feeling pretty good about my preaching," he said, "and I consider myself a very adaptable human being—having lived all over the world during my military service. But I have to tell you, preaching in my congregational context is one of the hardest adjustments I have ever had to make. Some of my people have a high school education or less. Some of them have never travelled outside the state. I read the *New Yorker* for enjoyment, and found that illustrations from that magazine worked well for the sermons I wrote in seminary. But here—forget it! My people don't even get the humor. In fact, I'm not sure they get the point of lots of my sermons. Some tell me I preach over their heads."

One of the cultural dilemmas that Bob and many new pastors face is that of being "cosmopolitans" who are called to preach within communities comprised primarily of "locals." Rather than equating the terms "local" and "cosmopolitan" with geographical areas (rural and urban respectively), sociologist Wade Clark Roof suggests that these terms refer to character types who can be found in a diversity of settings in the United States.[2] Locals are strongly oriented toward community or neighborhood, favor commitments to primary groups (family, neighborhood, fraternal and community organizations), tend to personalize their interpretations of social experience, and are more traditional in their beliefs and values. Cosmopolitans, on the other hand, are oriented toward the world outside the residential community, prefer membership in professional or special interest organizations, and are more open to social change and more tolerant of diversity in belief than locals. While a disproportionate number of locals are found in smaller communities, studies indicate that other factors—such as length of residence in a community, age, and educational level—play an even stronger role in determining orientation.

However one defines the terms, my own suspicion is that there are a number of cosmopolitan new clergy who are called, in their first pastorates, to serve congregations comprised primarily of locals. While the pastor's own global worldview and vision is one of the gifts she or he brings to the congregation through preaching, it may also be one of the factors that contributes to that startling gap initially experienced between preacher and people.

Crossing the Boundary between Seminary and Parish

The minister's own upbringing and pre-seminary acculturation are not the only factors that contribute to the cultural dislocation new clergy experience. A study undertaken by the Alban Institute indicates that seminary education itself may exacerbate ministerial culture shock by immersing future pastors in a set of values that are at odds with those values cherished by many local congregations. For example, while mainline seminaries typically value intellectual acumen, a liberal sociopolitical stance, competitive achievement, and a passive/dependent relationship between students and teacher, the fledgling pastor is often thrust into a parish setting in which practical skills, a conservative sociopolitical stance, collaboration in working with others, and a strong leadership style are valued.[3]

I still remember one of the parishioners in my dairy farming church commenting to me bluntly, but not unkindly, soon after my arrival: "Well, it's obvious from what we've seen about you and your husband on paper that you've got plenty of 'book sense.' That's great. But what this congregation usually wants to know about their pastors is: Do they have any 'common sense?'" His comments are reflective of the Alban Institute findings and are indicative of the value differences one encounters when moving from seminary to parish. Many a bright seminarian has had a tough go of it in the parish because "book sense" was not matched by "common sense" and people skills. Conversely, some of the finest pastors I have known never excelled in seminary academics, but greatly excelled in the kinds of practical Christian wisdom and human compassion that are valued in the parish.

One of the warnings seminarians typically receive from concerned church members is that they "not let that (highfalutin) seminary education ruin you as a minister." Often seminary faculty chuckle indulgently upon hearing this advice, perceiving it to be yet another instance of anti-intellectualism on the part of church members. However, the Alban study suggests that such "folk wisdom" may deserve a second hearing. Perhaps what is at the heart of this warning is not so much an anti-intellectualism as a deep-rooted awareness that the culture of the seminary and the culture of the church are different. Savvy church members know this truth, and are fearful that three or four years of immersion in the seminary environment can significantly alter a student's perception of the parish.

Culture Shock among Seasoned Pastors

But congregational culture shock is not the purview of new pastors alone; even the most seasoned clerics can find themselves reeling from its unexpected jolt. Witness these real-life vignettes. (Names and some details have been changed to insure anonymity.)

Valerie, pastor for six years in a successful suburban new church development effort (and, for many years previous, an overseas missionary of her denomination) responded to the call of an inner-city African American congregation to become its interim pastor. As a white, upper middle-class woman she openly spoke of her struggles to communicate the gospel effectively in her new environment.

"The culture shock," she admitted, "has been every bit as great as that which I experienced in going to the Far East from the U.S. as a missionary. At first I felt as though my sermons were boring this congregation to death. Then, I began reading more about preaching in the African American tradition. During the past few months I've even begun experimenting in my own preaching—using some of the cadences and rhetorical devices of the black tradition, and preaching entirely without notes. My congregation seems to love it. They appreciate my efforts to meet them where they are. But my husband has a tough time with it. He says I don't sound like myself any more when I preach."

Tim and Beth, a clergy couple, moved from their post as associate pastors in a highly educated and politically active urban congregation, to become co-pastors of a blue-collar congregation in a small town. "What we miss the most," said Beth, "are people like us that we can talk to about literature or politics or the challenges of juggling professional careers and family. We also miss the anonymity of the city. Whenever a car with out-of-town license plates shows up in our driveway, everybody in town wants to know whose it is!

"As for preaching," Beth continues, "you know how much I love poetry, and love to craft sermons that use a lot of poetic imagery and subtlety. I'm wondering if I can get away with that here. I'm wondering if people will even understand what I'm trying to say if I don't say it more simply and directly."

"The difficulty for our pastors," said In Soo, a Korean-American seminarian, "is that they are trying to minister to two very diverse cultures within one congregation: the culture of the immigrants, and the culture of their children and grandchildren. The first generation immigrants live in a land that doesn't exist any more: Korea of twenty-five years ago. They are steeped in Confucian thought modes, speak Korean language, and fear letting go of the past in order to make their

home in a country that regularly discriminates against them. They want to worship in the style to which they were accustomed in Korea, and are upset that their children and grandchildren are not more respectful and appreciative of their Korean ways.

"The second and third generations of Korean-American Christians, in contrast, speak English, are increasingly becoming Americanized, and are frustrated by their parents' and grandparents' orientation toward the past. Despite the marginalization and discrimination they experience in this culture, they are trying to make it their home. They find little meaning in the worship of their elders, and prefer to worship in more contemporary styles and forms.

"As a result, our congregations rarely worship with everyone together. The more common practice is that the senior pastor preaches for the Korean language service, and other pastors or seminarians are brought in to lead English-speaking services for youth and young adults. Most of the pastors I know would be very fearful of having to preach to the youth or children. It's not just the language gap. It's the tremendous cultural gap that exists between the generations."

"I learned the hard way what not to preach about in the retirement home," laughed Diane, a parish pastor turned chaplain. "Most of the residents were polite about it, but they also let me know in no uncertain terms that they are sick unto death of having younger people come in and preach to them about aging! As one woman pointedly said to me, 'We care about the same things everybody else does—politics, the economy, the latest church fights. Why don't you talk about those things when you preach? That would keep us interested.'"

These real-life vignettes give evidence that even the most experienced pastors can undergo culture shock when moving from one ministry setting to another, or when seeking to address divergent groups within a congregation. Unlike ministers of another era who often spent their entire ministerial careers among congregations in their own home states, pastors in our mobile, pluralistic society change positions frequently and may be called upon to preach in widely divergent settings during the course of a lifetime. The shifting contexts for ministry, and the shifting lifestyles, beliefs, and values encountered, can present significant challenges for communicating the gospel effectively.

Priestly Listening: Universals, Individuals, and Cultures

When pastors sit in their studies, studying the scriptures and preparing their sermons, they engage in what Leander Keck calls an act of "priestly listening"—"listening/hearing in solidarity with the people, vicariously . . . on behalf of the congregation."[4] Through empathetic imagination a pastor takes to the biblical text the questions, concerns, joys, and troubles of his or her particular congregation in order to discern, through the Spirit's guidance, a meaningful word to proclaim from the pulpit. However, as the examples above indicate, the imaginative and empathetic task of biblical interpretation in preaching can be complicated when the cultural "world" assumed by the preacher and the "world" assumed by the congregation differ.

Cultural anthropologists tell us that people are, in certain respects: (1) *like all others* (sharing certain universals with the whole human race); (2) *like no others* (having distinctive traits that mark them as individuals), and (3) *like some others* (sharing cultural traits with a particular group of people).[5] Each of these realities has significant implications for the preaching event.

Because people are, in certain respects, *like all others*, preachers can proclaim the gospel in a wide variety of settings with some assurance that (at least a degree of) effective, intelligible, and meaningful communication can occur. It is the very assumption that people share common emotional experiences (anger, joy, frustration, or despair), biological characteristics (being born helpless, needing food and drink for sustenance, aging, dying), or theological attributes (being created in the image of God, redeemed in Jesus Christ, and transformable through the workings of the Holy Spirit) that makes it possible for ministers to preach the gospel to people they do not know.

The fact that every individual is, in certain respects, *like no others* is an equally important consideration for the preacher. Parish pastors do not prepare their weekly sermons for generic humanity. They prepare sermons for particular individuals who populate their congregations and bring to the preaching event their own unique personalities, life circumstances, and concerns.

Thus the preacher who is also pastor sits in the study with the full awareness that Susan and Dave are on the brink of divorce, that Ida has just been informed that her cancer is terminal, that Ray is the latest victim of job loss due to corporate takeover, and that five-year-old Libby shows all the signs of being physically abused. The awareness of individual hearers and their real-life situations prevents the preacher from (mis)using the pulpit as a platform from which to voice abstract answers to abstract theological questions posed by an abstract (and faceless) humanity. The amorphous bones of universal humanity take on flesh and blood, personality and character, as the preacher grapples with issues of faith and life on behalf of particular individuals represented within the congregation.

Preaching at its best, however, is not only attentive to universal human concerns or to individual human needs and issues. Preaching also addresses groups of people—corporate bodies—who, in certain respects, are *like some others*. Preaching addresses "cultures" or "subcultures"—communities who share common lifestyles, assumptions, and values that both unite them with one another and that differentiate them from other such subgroups. When anthropologist Clifford Geertz defines "culture" he speaks of it as a vast communications network through which a group of people give expression in symbolic form to their own beliefs and values. Culture, he writes, is "an historically transmitted pattern of meanings embodied in symbols . . . by means of which [human beings] communicate, perpetuate, and develop their knowledge about and attitudes toward life."[6] By attending closely to the signs and symbols of its corporate life and by interpreting (and reinterpreting) their meaning, the student of a culture can discern what a community believes and values, what it is that gives one community its distinctive character in relation to another.

A focus upon the "cultural" in preaching pushes the pastor toward the kind of priestly listening that moves beyond the bounds of universals and individuals to consider communal traits and characteristics that unite members with one another and with other societal and ecclesial communities of belief and practice. A focus upon the cultural in preaching encourages the preacher to recognize that some of the "universals" she or he assumes in preaching may not be universals at all—but beliefs and values that are interpreted through a very particular cultural lens and vision. A focus upon the cultural in preaching encourages the preacher to address the congregation *as* congregation—a distinctive and unique community of faith that is, itself, in certain respects "like no others."[7]

The Cultural Worlds of Congregations

Congregations exist within an intricate and overlapping complex of cultures and their symbolic networks—cultures of both a societal and a churchly nature. For example, on the societal front all U.S. congregations participate to some degree in what we might term "the greater American culture." Any pastor who has struggled to proclaim the gospel faithfully during a time of national crisis or on the Sunday during the July Fourth weekend knows firsthand the significance that a shared U.S. cultural heritage can have for the preaching event.

In like manner one can appropriately speak on the churchly front of "the culture of Western Protestantism," or of "the ethos of the Reformed tradition." Congregations as ecclesial bodies also participate in larger communities of Christian faith and witness whose symbols, beliefs, and values they share.

However, it is also the case that within the pluralism of church and society in the United States there are many subgroups who, though sharing some of the patterns evidenced in a larger culture, also embody a very distinctive set of beliefs, values, and lifestyles that differentiate them from other groups within that culture. Anthropologists call such groups "subcultures,"[8] and cite a number of factors that contribute to their distinctiveness. Those factors include (but are not limited to) racial and ethnic heritage, geographical location, social class, age, and sex.

Pastors such as Al (leading worship in the prison), Valerie (ministering in an African American urban congregation), and Diane (a retirement home chaplain) are representative of clergy who lead worship in congregations where such societal subgroups are visibly represented. Each of them could speak appropriately (and respectively) of challenges confronted when preaching in the context of a prison subculture, an African American and urban subculture, or in the midst of a subculture of the aging.[9] Each of them is also preaching "across subcultures"—in the sense that the subculture in which each is most "at home" is different from the subculture in which she or he preaches.

However, while the term *subculture* has ordinarily been used in reference to larger *societal* groupings (whose influence may also be felt within churchly contexts), we have witnessed in this century a strong movement toward utilizing the term also in relation to *eccle-*

sial bodies. Theologian H. Richard Niebuhr was an early forerunner in this arena with his emphasis upon the subcultural nature of denominations. In his benchmark 1929 study, *The Social Sources of Denominationalism,* Niebuhr drew a compelling portrait of the interrelationships between societal subcultures and denominations in American life. Focusing upon four societal divisions—class, race, national origin, and regionalism—Niebuhr demonstrated the primacy of these factors in shaping America's denominational life.[10] It was social factors, Niebuhr argued, rather than religious factors, that contributed most to religious denominationalism in American society. Thus denominations themselves took on the characteristics of "subcultures."

In this new era of religious volunteerism, in which people switch from one denomination to another with relative freedom, the ascriptive forces that Niebuhr identified as shaping denominational life in the United States (race, region, class, and ethnicity) are eroding. However, the search for a place of subcultural belonging continues in American life. Many church members, who have intentionally chosen one denomination or Christian tradition over another, will testify that it was their own frustration with certain beliefs, values, and practices of their former denominational "subculture" that pushed them toward a new denomination where they feel more "at home."

Sociologists Wade Clark Roof and William McKinney contend that even though the link between societal and denominational subcultures has been weakened in mainline Protestantism in the United States, denominations still serve as "quasi-ethnic" groups of belonging and meaning-giving in American society, and can rightly be termed "subcultures."[11] It is the social behavior of religious groups—their actions, customs, and culture—and not just their words and stated beliefs that distinguish them from one another. "[I]ndividuals sharing a common outlook or behavioral style increasingly cluster around those institutions, officially or unofficially identified with constellations of moral values and styles with which they approve."[12]

The Congregation as Subculture

Yet it is also the case that the primary locus for Christian belonging and identity-formation in this age of mobility and religious volun-

teerism is not the denomination; it is the congregation. With the ero-
sion of denominational and other affiliative ties, mainline American
Christians increasingly seek a congregation where they are "at home"
or feel that they "belong." Consequently, it is not at all uncommon
for a person to belong to a Methodist congregation in one community, to join a Presbyterian church in another, and to worship with the
Baptists in a third.

Is it then in any way appropriate to call the congregation itself a
"subculture"? Over two decades ago, Christian educator C. Ellis Nelson paved the way for such consideration with his assertion that the
congregation is the "primary society of Christians"[13] that culturally
conditions its members in faith and life. By interpreting and communicating the biblical faith symbolically, said Nelson, congregations
shape the perceptions, consciences, and self-identification of individuals. "The congregation, then, is a school of faith. All that the congregation does is both a means of communicating the faith and a subject
of investigation."[14]

More recently James Hopewell has argued that congregations not
only can be, but ought to be viewed as subcultures.[15] Moving beyond
the ordinary usage of the term in regard to societal groups at large,
and even beyond its use in relation to denominations, Hopewell
maintains that congregations, too, are communities that embody
distinctive worldviews, values, and lifestyles. They too can be viewed
(following Geertz's lead) as communication networks, each having a
unique web of signs and symbols—a distinctive idiom—that binds
it together and distinguishes it from other congregations.

"Idiom," in this understanding, incorporates all the symbolic
forms by which a congregation communicates its own peculiar identity. It includes verbal symbols (such as stories and jokes, sermons,
favorite hymns, oral and written histories, and church publications)
and nonverbal symbols (such as ritual acts, architecture, gestures,
and visual arts). All are significant components of the symbolic language through which communities of faith give meaning and order
to their lives.

When people go church shopping, they tend to gravitate toward
churches in which they feel most "at home." In explaining why they
chose one congregation over another, parishioners will frequently
comment about characteristics such as the quality of warmth and
welcome they experienced, the caliber of worship, Christian educa-

tion or other programmatic offerings, the personalities of church leaders, or the nature of the church's mission involvement. What Hopewell would contend is that these characteristics are all a part of the church's unique idiom—the signs and symbols through which it communicates its distinctive subcultural identity. Through their own initial participation in the symbolic life of the congregation, visitors begin to perceive (even though they may not be able clearly to articulate it) something of the congregation's distinctive character. For, as Hopewell reminds us, "a congregation is held together by much more than creeds, governing structures and programs. At a deeper level, it is implicated in the symbols and signals of the world, gathering and grounding them in the congregation's own idiom."[16]

Further, as Hopewell demonstrates—and as I discovered first-hand in my multichurch parish—a comparative study of congregational idioms will reveal significant differences in the worldviews and values of congregations which appear, in terms of the ordinary societal and ecclesial distinctions (race, social status, geographical location, denominational affiliation) to be very similar.[17] Even among four congregations of similar size, located in the same geographical region and appearing (on the surface) to be similar in makeup, the pastor can encounter four very diverse subcultural idioms and ways of viewing and responding to the world. As we have seen before, pastoring four churches *is* a lot like having four children or (to use a less maternalistic image) four friends—each with his or her own distinctive personality.

Preaching as Cross-Cultural Communication

If Hopewell is correct, then the kinds of situations described thus far in this chapter are only the tip of the iceberg in terms of the subcultural diversity pastors encounter in preaching. When subculture is defined in terms of "idiom" (and not solely in terms of race, ethnicity, class, age, or geography), the possibility that a pastor will, at some time in the course of a ministerial career, be required to preach to people of a significantly different subculture is greatly expanded. Any notable idiomatic differences between pastor and people—whether due to societal, denominational, or congregational factors—has potential to create communicational difficulty in the pulpit.

Yet how does a pastor know whether she or he is preaching across subcultures? Where is the dividing line that separates "intracultural" (within one culture or subculture) preaching from "cross-cultural" or "intercultural" (between two or among several cultures) preaching?

When authors in the communication field discuss such matters, they point us away from using an "either/or" approach to culture and communication. Rather, they encourage us to view all human communication as resting on a continuum between cultural homogeneity and cultural heterogeneity.[18]

L. E. Sarbaugh, for example, cites a number of factors—psychological, social, and cultural—that contribute to the degree of "interculturality" experienced among communicators. Included in his list are elements such as number of persons involved in the communication event, perceived relationships among the participants, perceived intent of the communicators, verbal and nonverbal code systems, normative patterns of belief and overt behaviors, and worldview.[19] While all of these variables can contribute to the degree of communicational difficulty experienced among persons, Sarbaugh contends that worldview and values are the most stable, enduring, and difficult to modify.

If Sarbaugh's approach is applied to the instance of preaching, communication in the pulpit can also be seen as residing on a continuum between two poles. Preachers whose idioms, values, and worldviews are very different from those of their congregations will have to reckon with a higher degree of interculturality in their preaching than will those who are preaching to people whose subculture is more consonant with their own.

Viewing preaching according to its degree of interculturality also highlights the reality that, in at least minor ways, preaching across subcultures is a concern for *most* clergy. Few of us (thank God!) are preaching to people who are just like us. Furthermore, congregations themselves are not as homogenous subculturally as Hopewell's approach would suggest. Many congregations—while loosely held together by a common "idiom"—are also internally divided along other subcultural lines. The wise pastor will attend not only to the subculture of the congregation as a whole, but also to the diverse (and sometimes competing) subcultures that coexist within a congregation.

The Homiletical Need

Certainly it is the case that many clergy become acquainted over time and through various means with the particular idioms and subcultural identities of their congregations. Through informal as well as formal means, pastors come to "know" their congregations.[20] Some pastors actually become multicultural, able to live and function with ease in several subcultural contexts. Yet it is also the case that many pastors attain their subcultural knowledge of congregations in a tacit and haphazard fashion, and lack appropriate methods or procedures to aid their discernment.

As for preaching itself, many pastors discover that while it is relatively easy to adjust their sermons in regard to surface subcultural issues (for example, to tailor vocabulary or use of colloquialisms toward the understanding and usage of a particular congregation), it is far more difficult to identify and attend to those subtler and deeper subcultural attitudes, values, and patterns of thought and action that also have an impact upon the "fittingness" of a sermon.

Pastors need explicit skills and training in "exegeting congregations" and their subcultures—just as they need skills and training in exegeting the Scriptures. (What is distinctive about a particular congregation's subcultural identity? How does one go about reading the signs and symbols of congregational life in order to discern congregational worldview, values, and ethos? Are there any paradigms by which a local pastor can distinguish between his or her own subcultural understandings and those of the congregation?)

Pastors also need help reflecting upon the significance of congregational subculture for the entire text-to-sermon process. How can preaching—in both its theology and its art—be both "fitting" for a local community of faith and also "transformative" according to the message of the gospel? (Of what import is congregational subculture for the selection of texts for preaching? the questions and concerns the pastor takes to the text on behalf of a community? the theological "slant" taken in the sermon? the communicational strategy adopted for proclaiming the message? the design and form of the sermon? the use of language within the sermon? the selection of appropriate examples and illustrations for the sermon?)

Unfortunately, pastors who turn to homiletical texts for help in these areas are likely to be disappointed. While many homileticians do recognize that congregations "matter" in the preaching event, they usually fall short of providing the pastor with either a workable model for identifying and analyzing congregational subcultural differences, or with an adequate discussion of the import of congregational particularity for the theological construction and artistic design of the sermon.

The Homiletical Void

As early as the fifth century, Augustine, the author of the Christian church's first homiletical textbook, recognized that the particular sociocultural makeup of a congregation should influence the minister as preacher or teacher. He wrote:

> It likewise makes a great difference . . . whether there are few or many; whether learned or unlearned, or a mixed audience made up of both classes; whether they are townsfolk or countryfolk, or both together; or a gathering in which all sorts and conditions of [humanity] are represented. For it cannot fail to be the case that different persons should affect in different ways the one who intends to instruct orally and likewise the one who intends to give a formal discourse. . . .[21]

However, pastors of the late twentieth century who turn to contemporary preaching texts—either for help in the "exegesis" of their congregations or for guidance in preaching more effectively in diverse congregational contexts—are likely to be disappointed. While contemporary homiletics has not ignored the listeners in the preaching event, preaching texts have tended to focus more attention upon the universals of human experience or upon the psychological needs and filters individual hearers bring to the preaching event, than they have upon congregations as corporate communities with distinctive subcultural identities.

For example, in David Buttrick's *Homiletic* the focus is clearly upon the universals of human experience. Assuming that all humans share certain "structures of human consciousness," (or "fields of awareness")[22] Buttrick's primary concern is how sermons can be shaped so that "the structure of the [biblical] text, playing across time, will form a structure of [theological] understanding in our twentieth-century consciousness that will be different from the original meaning, but which will be structured similarly."[23] So strongly does Buttrick stress the commonality of human "structures of consciousness" that he altogether blurs any cultural distinctions that might exist either among congregations or between pastor and congregation. Indeed, Buttrick openly argues that congregational exegesis has little value for the preacher.

> Normally, books on homiletics spend pages speaking about the character of a congregation, particularly when discussing situational preaching. We have not. While ministers will plan sermons as systems intending toward a particular congregational consciousness, usual discussions of congregation may not be helpful—they tend to separate minister and congregation. The idea that there is a people whose mind and ethos can be understood, so that a minister may teach, or convert, or empathize with, or whatever, is not a helpful way of thinking. Instead, we have tried to link our consciousness with congregational consciousness, our world with their world, so that preaching may speak in a shared consciousness.[24]

On the other end of the spectrum, a variety of homiletical texts written since the 1960s and informed by the fields of psychology and communication theory, have focused upon preaching and pastoral concerns. (See, for example, Edgar Jackson, *A Psychology for Preaching*; Merrill Abbey, *Communication in Pulpit and Parish*; Clement Welsh, *Preaching in a New Key*; Donald Capps, *Pastoral Counseling and Preaching*; and J. Randall Nichols, *Building the Word* and *The Restoring Word*.) The emphasis in these works is upon individual hearers and the particular filters, needs, and resistances they bring to the communication event of preaching. Consequently, preaching is viewed an act of pastoral care through which listeners can find wholeness and restoration for their lives. Or, as J. Randall Nichols succinctly states it, "Healing is the point."[25]

There is no question the local pastor has been helped by homiletical resources that focus upon psychological and communicational dimensions of the preaching task. Healing is indeed *one* of the points of preaching, and the wise preacher exercises a great deal of pastoral care through proclamation.

Healing is not the *only* point, however. Faithful proclamation will also engage its hearers as a corporate body in ethical reflection upon their corporate engagement within a larger church and society. Unless a focus on the individual is balanced by an equally strong focus upon the corporate and communal nature of Christian procla-

mation, sermons may well reflect, rather than challenge, the individ-
ualistic and therapeutic approach to life Robert Bellah and his colleagues already find so rampant in American culture.[26]

Voices in the Wilderness

One contemporary homiletician who has long recognized the significance of culture for preaching, and who has written extensively
about preaching in the African American tradition, is Henry H.
Mitchell. In his book *Black Preaching*, Mitchell focuses upon the
unique dynamics of preaching within the African American church
tradition in America.[27] Taking the subcultural dimensions of African
American societal and congregational life very seriously, Mitchell
contends that the success of black preachers has been in large part
due to their ability to preach, theologically and communicationally,
in a style consonant with the subculture of their hearers.

In *The Recovery of Preaching*, Mitchell argues that white preachers
have much to learn from the black tradition of "preaching as folk culture."[28] In part, says Mitchell, the downfall of American white middle-class preaching has to do with the inability of its preachers to
proclaim the gospel in the idiom of the people. Unlike black preaching, which "has never tried to wage a major war against the culture of
the masses of folk,"[29] "White middle-class Protestant preaching . . .
has been carried on in an academically oriented counterculture to
the folk idiom of America's majority."[30] If white preachers would
communicate more effectively with their congregations, they should
learn to speak in the cultural terms of their people.

> Whether in the Black ghetto, the affluent suburb, or the uttermost
> parts of the earth, the deepest and most meaningful cultural heritage
> of persons must be identified, respected, and built upon. . . . Preaching
> that makes meaningful impact on lives has to reach persons at gut
> level, and it is at this level of communally stored wisdom and cultural
> affinity that such access to living souls is gained.[31]

One of the most promising indications that North American
homileticians are finally beginning to heed Mitchell's advice and pay
more attention to the folk cultures of their people has been the pub-
lication of *Preaching as a Social Act: Theology and Practice*.[32] Edited by
Arthur Van Seters and incorporating chapters by eight homileticians

and theologians, this work explores how the social loci of biblical text, preacher, and congregation inevitably influence the theology and practice of preaching.

Here Walter Brueggemann reminds us that the biblical text and its meanings never simply exist; they are always being produced through the engagement of a community with that text. From the initial canonical formation of the text, to its interpretation by the preacher, to its reception and hearing by the congregation, meaning is being created and recreated. Thus,

> The sermon is not an act of reporting on an old text, but it is an act of making a new text visible and available. This new text in part is the old text, and in part is the imaginative construction of the preacher which did not exist until the moment of utterance by the preacher.[33]

Don Wardlaw's chapter on the congregation and its role as "corporate agent" in the act of preaching begins to explore some of the avenues open to the preacher for congregational sociocultural exegesis, and urges preachers toward greater concern for the congregation as corporate hearer in the sermon formation process.[34] And Edwina Hunter calls preachers to become more self-conscious and reflective about their own social and spiritual formation and how it influences their proclamation.[35]

However, by its very nature (essays written by a variety of authors) this work falls short of providing the local pastor with either an exegetical procedure for interpreting congregations or with a cohesive model for integrating subcultural concerns in the hermeneutics of preaching. It is a good step in the right direction, but further steps need to be taken.

The truth is that if one scans the American homiletical scene of the last several decades for works specifically devoted to preaching and subcultural contexts, the landscape is rather arid. A few lone voices have tried to increase concern for preaching's cultural contexts, but so far relatively few have joined their homiletical chorus.

Preaching Courses and Textbooks

The real "rub," of course, comes in seminary preaching courses which typically devote far more attention to the exegesis of biblical texts than they do to the exegesis of congregations and their contexts. The assumption is (erroneously) made that while students need well-defined procedures for exegeting the Scriptures, they can rely on intuition and instinct alone for exegeting congregations. The sad result is that students and pastors tend to commit one of three errors in preaching:

1. They prepare generic sermons for generic humanity that never truly become enfleshed in the real-life situations of particular congregations. (How often I have heard students in preaching class announce, despite strong encouragement that they prepare their sermons with a particular congregation in mind, that the sermon "could have been preached to any congregation anywhere.")
2. They paint overly simplistic pictures of their hearers in preaching, attributing to them attitudes, beliefs, or values that they do not actually hold. (As I have observed contemporary parish preaching, this proclivity is a common one. Preachers frequently create flat "straw figures" in their sermons, whose lives and attitudes do not accurately reflect the more ambiguous nature of life as their hearers experience it. Example: "We are *all* like the Pharisees. We *always* want public acclaim for the good works we do, and are unhappy unless we get it.")
3. They project onto congregations—unconsciously and unintentionally—their own issues and concerns. (I remember preaching a sermon in my rather sedentary rural parish entitled "To Move or To Stay Put," based on the story of Abraham and Sarah in Genesis 12. I was startled into recognizing the ways in which I had projected my own life issues onto the congregation when a member perceptively commented on her way out the door that morning, "Thinking about leaving us, are you?")

While the best textbooks on the contemporary homiletical scene discourage such pitfalls, they also fall short of providing pastors with a methodology for congregational "exegesis" or with adequate discussions of how the preacher navigates the difficult waters of cross-cultural communication of the gospel. We turn now to a consideration of two such texts, written by two of the foremost thinkers on the contemporary homiletical scene: Thomas G. Long's *The Witness of Preaching* and Fred B. Craddock's *Preaching*.

Thomas G. Long, *The Witness of Preaching*

Thomas G. Long is a strong proponent for integrating congregational considerations throughout the text-to-sermon process. Indeed, one of Long's primary concerns is that sermon preparation not be viewed as a two-stage process in which the pastor first exegetes the biblical text, and then exegetes the congregation in order to *apply* biblical insights. Rather, Long advocates an interpretive approach in which the pastor, in a priestly way, *represents* the congregation—its wishes, hopes, hurts, concerns, and dreams—in each stage of the hermeneutical process. He writes,

> The preacher goes to the biblical text for the congregation and, indeed, with the congregation. . . . Exegesis is a work of the church enacted through the preacher as its chosen representative. . . .
>
> So the move from text to sermon begins, not with a decision about how to inform the congregation about the results of the preacher's personal exegesis of the text but, rather, a decision about what aspect of the congregation-text encounter will be carried over into the sermon itself. The bridge the preacher must now cross is the one between the text-in-congregational-context and the sermon-in-congregational-context.[36]

Consequently, the method Long outlines for biblical exegesis and the model he provides for sermon construction incorporate congregational concerns at each juncture. In biblical exegesis the preacher is advised "to survey the congregation in the imagination's eye" and to "ask the questions they would ask" or "the questions they may not dare to ask" of the text.[37] "Focus" and "function" statements (which articulate respectively the central theological affirmation of the sermon and the sermon's intended "affect" upon the hearers) are to be prepared with specific congregations in mind, acknowledging that a shift in congregational context may well necessitate a shift in sermonic focus and function.[38] Illustrations and examples are to be selected which can address and are reflective of the diversity of life situations and experiences congregants bring to the preaching event.[39]

In order to foster identification with the hearers, Long encourages pastors to be as honest as possible about their own struggles and life issues,[40] to visualize the congregation that will be present when the sermon is preached, and actually to include congregation members in the sermon-writing process through group Bible study of upcoming sermonic texts. However, where Long falls short is in providing the pastor with methods for "exegeting" the congregation in all its sociocultural particularity so that the preacher as "priest" *can* best represent it in the homiletical process. While Long devotes an entire chapter to a discussion of "Biblical Exegesis for Preaching,"[41] there is no corresponding chapter in his work devoted to congregational or contextual exegesis for preaching. Although Long acknowledges, "Many other methods are available to bring the questions, needs, and insights of the congregation into the preacher's awareness as the text is encountered," *The Witness of Preaching* does not include a fuller exposition of these methods.

In the same way that methods of biblical exegesis can help prevent the "eisegesis" of Scripture texts, so congregational exegesis can help curb the tendency of the preacher to "eisegete" the congregation. Pastors are in need of methods and procedures which can assist them in this interpretive act. While Long is absolutely correct that congregational exegesis should not be considered a "second step" in the homiletical process, congregational interpretation is a necessary "first step" (as well as an ongoing process) through which the pastor can listen attentively in order to deepen his/her understanding of the congregation *on its own terms.*

Fred B. Craddock, *Preaching*

In *Preaching* (as in *As One Without Authority* and *Overhearing the Gospel*), Fred Craddock is not only concerned for the preaching of the Word, but also for the hearing of it. "However one may define the Word of God," says Craddock, "this expression must be included: 'it is fitting.' The old Anglo-Saxon word 'meet,' as in 'meet and right so to do,' captured the idea precisely: the Word meets the listener; contact is made."[42]

Craddock views the sermon preparation process as taking place in two separate and distinct stages: interpretation (determining the message, what the preacher will say), and sermon design (determining how to communicate the message). The "interpretation," or hermeneutical stage, necessarily involves a dual focus: interpretation of the *listeners*, "including their contexts: personal, domestic, social, political, economic,"[43] and interpretation of the *biblical text* in its contexts—historical, theological, and literary.

In what may well be one of the most strongly and eloquently worded pleas for "exegeting the congregation" in current homiletical literature, Craddock writes:

> Giving disciplined time and attention to the interpretation of one's listeners is critical for preaching. It in no way diminishes the importance of careful exegesis of texts, but then neither does any amount of work in a text make a sermon apart from this understanding. No book of theology, even if it is addressed to the modern mind; no biblical commentary, even if it moves the text toward the pulpit; no volume of sermons, packaged and ready for delivery, has the Word winged for the hearts and minds of a particular group of listeners. Only the minister there can properly do that.[44]

How does a pastor get to know the listeners as "congregation" so that the Word can take root and grow in local soil? Craddock recommends three strategies: formal, informal, and empathetic imagination.[45]

Formally, the pastor gets to know a congregation by reading histories of the church and the region in which it is located, attending to local newspaper accounts of life and death rituals in the community, and conducting key interviews with community and church leaders. *Informally*, the pastor serves, on a daily basis, as a listening and observing participant in the ongoing life and activities of a congregation and a community. Through *empathetic imagination*, defined as "the capacity to achieve a large measure of understanding of another person without having had that person's experiences,"[46] pastors are enabled to envision all sorts of experiences they have not personally had and thereby are enabled to preach to people in many different stations in life.[47] In each instance the goal is not a surface observation or description of the listeners, but a more in-depth understanding of "the currents of a community's life, its ways of relating to itself and to the world, its values, and the images of its fears and hopes," which "enables the minister to interpret the listeners to themselves and hold their lives under the judgment and blessing of the gospel."[48]

Clearly, Craddock is a strong advocate for congregational exegesis and interpretation in preaching. The very structure and ordering of his chapters in the "Interpretation" section of his textbook ("Interpretation: The Listeners" [chap. 5], "Interpretation: The Text" [chap. 6], "Interpretation: Between Text and Listener" [chap. 7]) is revelatory of Craddock's firm commitment to a hermeneutical process for preaching which is, from beginning to end, bifocal. His suggested modes for congregational exegesis are reasonable, given the constraints of parish ministry, and his affirmation of what is possible through "empathetic imagination" is encouraging for those who find themselves preaching across subcultures.

However, there are also gaps in Craddock's approach. While he emphasizes the importance of knowing the hearers "both as individuals and as social units,"[49] Craddock does not always adequately differentiate between the two. Rather, his major differentiation is between attending to the listeners as *audience* "as a guest preacher would see them" (with attendant emphasis on the universals of human experience) and attending to the listeners as *congregation* "as a pastor knows them" (with emphasis on both the individual and sociocultural aspects of congregational life). The result is that congregational "cultures" or "subcultures" receive little explicit attention.

More important, however, is the reality that while Craddock offers a well-defined "procedure" for biblical interpretation, his three "methods" for congregational exegesis (formal, informal, and empathetic imagination) are more suggestive and descriptive in nature. To be sure, the task of congregational exegesis is of a different ilk than that of biblical exegesis, and necessarily occurs in a somewhat less structured and less defined manner. However, pastors who are seeking to understand the subcultures of their congregations would be aided by more fully defined and detailed "formal" and "informal" procedures than Craddock gives.

Conversation Partners, Old and New

What current preaching theory lacks, then, is any in-depth exploration of the nature of congregational "subcultures" and the roles they can and should play in the formation of sermons in local congregational contexts. What are some of the distinguishing characteristics of congregational subcultures, and by what method(s) can the local pastor gain a deeper understanding of them? Are there any paradigms by which a local pastor can distinguish between his or her own subcultural understandings and those of the congregation? How can the pastor bring biblical text and subcultural context together in the sermon toward the end that the sermon—in both its theology and its art—is more fitting and more transformative for a local community of faith?

While it is true that scholars in the field of preaching have not long or adequately attended to the role of congregational subculture and its impact upon preaching, there are two fields of inquiry—one old, and one new—that promise to be fruitful conversation partners for preaching as it grapples with such matters.

The first is the field of *cross-cultural missions.* On a far more global and cross-cultural (as opposed to cross-subcultural) level, authors in the field of international missions have struggled for decades to discern how expatriates serving in diverse cultures can give voice to theologies that are both "faithful" to Scripture and tradition and also "fitting" for a particular people. More recently, the emergence of indigenous local theologies around the world (such as *minjung* theology in South Korea, Latin American theologies of liberation, and feminist, Native American, and African American theologies in the United States) has challenged and stretched our thinking about the contextualization of theology. How does the local cultural community of faith itself contribute to the shaping of theology that is both fitting and faithful? By what norms or standards do we discern what "fitting" and "faithful" mean in diverse cultural contexts?

Rather than reinventing the cross-cultural wheel, homiletics would do well to attend to some of the conversations already under way regarding the contextualization of theology on a global level, and to reflect—in light of such discussions—upon appropriate methods for shaping contextual sermons in the congregational locale. Constructing appropriate sermons for and with rural churches in central Virginia is not unlike constructing appropriate theologies for and with base communities in Latin America. Though the contexts are different, many of the interpretive and communicational issues are similar.

The second field of inquiry that holds promise for a consideration of preaching and its subcultures is the newly emerging field of *congregational studies.* Although researchers have been using the tools of the social sciences to study congregations for over eighty years, it has only been in the last decade that an integrative field of inquiry known as "congregational studies" has begun to find its own voice on the American scene.[50]

Congregational studies is an interdisciplinary field that weds the social sciences (cultural anthropology, sociology, social psychology, organizational development) and theology in a effort to gain a better understanding of congregational identity and action. Rather than approaching the study of congregations by way of intuition or random investigation, authors in the field of congregational studies urge pastors and lay persons toward a more systematic approach to the exegesis of congregations.

Jackson Carroll, one of the authors of the very practical *Handbook for Congregational Studies*, has identified four possible entry points and foci for congregational analysis:

1. *Program.* "Those organizational structures, plans and activities through which a congregation expresses its mission and ministry both to its own members and those outside the membership;"
2. *Process.* "The underlying flow and dynamics of a congregation that knit it together in its common life and affect its morale and climate;"
3. *Social context.* "The setting, local and global, in which a congregation finds itself and to which it responds," and
4. *Identity.* "The persistent set of beliefs, values, patterns, symbols, stories and style that make a congregation distinctively itself."[51]

While each of these four dimensions is important for a full understanding of the congregation (and while all of them together cannot exhaust the mysterious workings of the Spirit in congregational life), it is the dimension of *identity* that is of particular concern to the cross-cultural preacher. By carefully attending to that "persistent set of beliefs, values, patterns, symbols, stories and style that make a congregation distinctively itself," the local pastor can deepen understanding regarding the operative assumptions that consciously or unconsciously inform a congregation's attitudes and actions. Congregational studies—particularly as informed by cultural anthropology and sociology—offers valuable assistance to the local pastor who is seeking to better understand and preach within the "strange new world" of an alien congregation.

Conclusion

For many pastors—new and seasoned—the task of preaching in the congregational context is closely akin to that of the foreign missionary; that is, they are communicating the gospel to gatherings of people whose idioms, worldviews, and values are significantly different from their own. Indeed, odds are quite good, given the ever-increasing mobility and plurality of American culture, that the multicultural challenges faced by local pastors will only increase with the passage of time.

However, unlike the cross-cultural missionary, who usually receives some training and orientation before she or he is thrust into a strange new world, preachers can be caught unaware and unprepared. *Unaware* because it is easy to assume that people who speak the same language and live in the same country and belong to the same denomination as we do are, to a large extent, "like" us. And *unprepared* because, on the whole, seminary courses and texts in homiletics have not adequately acknowledged the cross-cultural dimensions of the preaching task, and have frequently done a far better job of training future pastors to exegete Scripture than of teaching them to "exegete" and probe the depths of hidden meaning within local congregations and their subcultures.

The time is ripe for preaching texts and courses to acknowledge the cultural—in addition to the universal and individual—dimensions of the preaching task, to provide pastors and students with viable and workable procedures for congregational exegesis in the parish, and to explore more fully the nature of preaching as a highly contextual act of theological construction in the congregational context. It is the goal of this book to provide an initial foray into these areas, and to assist pastors in moving toward proclamation that is not only faithful to the gospel of Jesus Christ, but also fitting for local communities of faith. The goal is a worthy one. For, as Fred Craddock so rightly observes,

> Whatever may be provided a preacher by any and all resources, it is only when local soil has been added that the sermon will take root and grow. Such work is blessed by the Holy Spirit with the result that each one hears in his or her own language (Acts 2:6-8).[52]

2
Aiming toward Contextual Preaching

In the introduction to his book *Models of Contextual Theology,* Roman Catholic theologian Stephen Bevans tells of an experience he had as a theology student in Rome in the late 1960s that awakened him to the significance of culture for the shaping of theology for proclamation. It was the season of Advent, and Bevans, a twenty-something member of the Beatles generation, prepared a homily which explored the image of Christ as "sun." He began the homily with the playing of the Beatles' song, "Here Comes the Sun," and then elaborated upon the One who brings light and warmth to a cold and God-less world.

"I was very enthusiastic about what I said," reports Bevans, "and thought I had really done a good job of interpreting a traditional Christian symbol in contemporary terms."[1] Until, that is, an Indian participant in the liturgy approached Bevans and told him that Christ as sun was not a helpful image in his own context. The worshipper explained that in India the sun is an enemy that brings unbearable heat, terrible thirst, and the possibility of sunstroke. Rather than seeking and awaiting the coming of the sun, Indian people seek the shade as a respite from its dangerous rays.

"This incident," says Bevans, "was my first encounter with the fact that some of our predominantly western and northern liturgical and theological images are meaningless in other cultural contexts. I had read about this fact in books. I had heard other people talk about it in conversations, *but this was the first time that I had ever met someone who simply had no use for an idea that really meant something to me and was deeply nourishing, both theologically and spiritually.*"[2]

One of the realities encountered by contemporary pastors who are preaching the gospel in congregations whose cultures or subcultures are significantly different from their own is that they, too, can find themselves preaching something that is, to them, deeply meaningful, but that fails to feed the hearts and spirits of their hearers. The rural pastor who discovers that his favorite *New Yorker* cartoon depicting contemporary life fails to elicit even a chuckle in his congregational context; the lover of poetry whose use of a favorite poem in her blue-collar community draws blank stares; the occasional prison preacher whose pithy theological insight (which went over quite well in the local congregation) is answered with a resounding "Bull——!" in the prison—all know the frustration of discovering that what feeds them (spiritually and theologically) doesn't necessarily provide adequate or appropriate nutrition for their congregations.

Rather than recognizing that the challenge is one of transversing cultures in their proclamation, however, preachers may be tempted to cast blame elsewhere, either on their congregations (for a lack of appreciation for "good preaching"), or—quite commonly—on themselves (for their own inability to proclaim the gospel in a meaningful way for their people). Indeed, I am convinced that some pastors—especially pastors in new or significantly intercultural settings—are overly hard on themselves regarding their preaching. They judge as "poor" sermons that might well be judged differently if preached in an alternative context. The difficulty lies not so much with poor preaching (theologically, imagistically, communicationally) as with a lack of contextual "fit" between the sermon and the hearers.

Just as there is nothing intrinsically "poor" about the Advent image of Christ as sun (indeed, it is an image which has been found to be meaningful in a diversity of contexts throughout the history of the church), so the cartoon, poem, and insight cited above may also prove to be deeply meaningful when used in alternative contexts. Problems arise when they are used in cultural contexts in which a readily shared constellation of meanings via these signs and symbols cannot be assumed—that is, in contexts in which there is a high degree of interculturality between pastor and people.

The Goal: Contextual Preaching

Our quest, then, is for preaching that is more intentionally *contextual* in nature—that is, preaching which not only gives serious attention to the interpretation of biblical texts, but which gives equally serious attention to the interpretation of congregations and their sociocultural contexts; preaching which not only aims toward greater "faithfulness" to the gospel of Jesus Christ, but which also aims toward greater "fittingness" (in content, form and style) for a particular congregational gathering of hearers.

Missiologist Stephen Bevans has defined "contextual" theology as a way of doing theology in which one takes into account four things: "the spirit and message of the gospel; the tradition of the Christian people; the culture in which one is theologizing; and social change in that culture. . . ."[3] However, as we have already observed, recent homiletical theory has tended to give more attention to the spirit and message of the gospel (via extensive treatments of biblical exegetical methods) or to "tradition" (as defined by denominational or ecumenical doctrine) than it has to congregational cultures and subcultures—including their dynamics of social change and the more local "traditions" and belief systems to which they already subscribe.

Our aim is to tilt the scales in a more balanced direction—pressing toward greater recognition of the role congregational culture should play in sermonic theologizing, while, at the same time, not sacrificing "the spirit and message of the gospel." To sound such a call is not to advocate localism or creeping parochialism. Rather, it is to assert, in faith, that preaching can be both local in its address and global in its vision, both fitting for a particular congregation of God's people and faithful to a transformative gospel.

Indeed, in calling preachers toward greater contextuality in proclamation we are not advocating a new agenda for proclamation. Rather, we are calling for a return to some of Christian preaching's most ancient practices. A return to the spirit of Jesus whose own proclamation of God's reign was marked by its fittingness for farmers and fisherfolk, for servants and landowners, for Pharisees and tax collectors. A return to the spirit of Pentecost when a multicultural and multinational gathering of persons exclaimed, "Are not all these who are speaking Galileans? And how is it that we hear, each of us, in our own native language?"[4] A return to the spirit of Paul who was able to bring the Good News to Jew and Gentile, Jerusalem and Athens, through his own highly contextual proclamation. And a return to the spirit of countless faithful local pastors—pastors whose names will never be widely known, but who are valued by their congregations as preachers who have lived with them, known them,

loved them, and enfleshed the gospel in their midst in locally transformative ways.

Contextuality may be a new term on the theological horizon, but
it bespeaks a very old reality. We turn now to a consideration of some
of the theological reasons why its concerns are critical for more effective preaching in diverse congregational contexts.

Why Greater Contextuality in Preaching?
A Theological Apologetic

*1. Contextualization helps preachers remove "false stumbling blocks" to
the hearing of the gospel in their proclamation.*

In the closing chapter of *Theology of Culture*, Paul Tillich asks the
question: "How shall the [Christian] message . . . be focused for the
people of our time? . . . How do we make the message heard and seen,
and then either rejected or accepted?"[5] Tillich hastens to add that the
question for those who preach and teach *cannot* be: "How do we
communicate the gospel so that others will accept it? For this there is
no method." Acceptance or rejection of the gospel is beyond our control as preachers, and has to do with the workings of the Holy Spirit
in the lives of hearers. However, says Tillich, we who preach can strive
to communicate the gospel so as to make possible "a genuine decision . . . one based on understanding and on partial participation."[6]

In this discussion, Tillich makes a very helpful distinction between
"genuine" and "wrong" stumbling blocks in proclamation. It is of the
nature of the gospel itself to be a "genuine" stumbling block to hearers, says Tillich. That is, any message that has at its center a crucified
messiah, requires its adherents to love their enemies, and pronounces
it easier for a camel to get through the eye of a needle than for a rich
person to enter the realm of heaven is intrinsically offensive. While
such stumbling blocks may indeed lead to a rejection of the gospel
message, they are obstacles the preacher dare not remove in proclamation. To remove them is to disfigure the gospel itself.

There are, however, other stumbling blocks that occur in preaching: "wrong" stumbling blocks that are occasioned by the humanness
of the preaching event and inadequacies of communication on the
part of the preacher. Examples might include the use of theological
jargon which is empty of meaning for the hearers, the employment of
a sermon structure that is too complicated and obtuse for the hearers

to follow, or the use of images and illustrations that fail to embody the gospel in a believable way for a particular culture or faith community. These stumbling blocks impede a full hearing of the gospel and create unnecessary obstacles for those who would like to make a genuine decision concerning it. The preacher should make every effort to remove them. The challenging note on which Tillich ends his book is: "Will the Christian churches be able to remove the wrong stumbling blocks in their attempts to communicate the Gospel?"[7]

Tillich's challenge to the churches is still valid today when clear and intelligible proclamation of the gospel in a mode that leads to genuine hearing and decision-making is at a premium. In the first instance, preaching needs to become more contextualized in our day *not* in order to make the gospel more palatable, more appealing, or even more persuasive (despite encouragement from some quarters to do so). Preaching needs to attend more carefully to cultural context in order that the gospel may be more clearly heard and understood by all sorts of people in all sorts of settings.

The Reformed theological tradition, of which I am an heir, has long placed emphasis upon proclamation that is simple, direct, authentic, and clear.[8] John Calvin himself was a superb explicator of Scripture because he was a master of paraphrase, able to translate Scripture with precision and clarity into the common human discourse of his own time.[9] Yet contextualization emphasizes the reality that what is perceived to be "simple, direct, authentic, and clear" varies from congregation to congregation. It urges the preacher toward greater familiarity with congregational subcultures in order that she or he may more self-consciously avoid creating false stumbling blocks for the hearing of the gospel.

2. Contextualization in proclamation reflects the "accommodating" way in which God has dealt with humanity in revelation.

One of the themes that is never directly addressed by John Calvin but that is woven throughout his writing is an emphasis on the "accommodation" of God to human beings. For Calvin, the term *accommodation* does not have the negative overtones often attributed to it in current theological discussions. (That is, it does not imply a "selling out to culture" or false syncretism of the gospel with culture.) Rather, Calvin speaks of "accommodation" as being a part of God's gracious divine action through which God takes the initiative and rhetorically bridges—through word and deed—the great gulf that exists between human beings and God.[10]

For Calvin, this accommodation of God to humanity is first witnessed in creation itself. "God clothes, so to speak, His [sic] invisible, inaccessible nature with the visible, palpable raiment of the universe in which we live. In these lineaments small or vast—yet still finite— He condescends to our *captus*."[11] Scripture, in which "divinely appointed human authors and expositors . . . express and expound the divine rhetoric under the Spirit's guidance for the benefit of all,"[12] is another instance of God's accommodating ways toward humans. Indeed, Calvin (like Origen and Augustine before him) frequently appeals to the principle of accommodation as an apologetic device to explain seemingly inconsistent or contradictory passages within Scripture.

In like manner, Calvin views the incarnation as God's ultimate accommodating act: "In Christ God so to speak makes himself little in order to lower himself to our capacity, and Christ alone calms our consciences that they may dare intimately approach God."[13] Finally, the Lord's Supper is viewed by Calvin as an accommodating act in which the spiritual and physical are inextricably yoked. The sacrament is to be seen as "neither accommodation of physical to spiritual nor of spiritual to physical. It is rather accommodation of spiritual *in* physical."[14]

One of the benefits of Calvin's emphasis on "accommodation" is that it reminds us that revelation in preaching can never be earned or deserved or attained by our own human striving. It is always a gift of a God who chooses, in freedom, to reveal Godself to us—to condescend to our *captus* (comprehension). As every preacher knows, there are times when our finest efforts fall flat and times when our poorest sermons (the ones we are embarrassed to preach) take wing, through the Spirit's stirrings, and soar. We cannot orchestrate God's appearing in our midst.

But Calvin also reminds us of a reality that sometimes got lost in neo-orthodox understandings of preaching: namely, that revelation never comes to human beings in other than a mediated form. In revelation spiritual and physical, divine and human, are always yoked. As in sacraments so in preaching, the eternal revelation of God and human words unite to become, by the Spirit's act, a revelatory act. Even if revelation is "from above," the Word did become *flesh*. And in every aspect of preaching—content, form, language, delivery, style—the sermon must do so as well.

Dietrich Bonhoeffer, who held a highly sacramental view of proclamation, paints in his Finkenwald lectures a portrait of preaching that holds in tension both the movement and action of God when the Word is proclaimed, and the accommodation of God to our human situation. "The proclaimed word is the incarnate Christ himself . . . it is the Christ himself walking through his congregation as the Word," Bonhoeffer asserts.[15] Yet Bonhoeffer hastens to add that in preaching we also witness Christ *bearing human nature.*

> The word of the sermon intends to accept [hu]mankind, nothing else. It wants to bear the whole of human nature. In the congregation all sins would be cast upon the Word. Preaching must be done so that the hearer places all of his [or her] needs, cares, fears, and sins upon the Word. The Word accepts all of these things. When preaching is done in this way, it is the proclamation of Christ.[16]

Contextualization urges preaching to claim its human as well as its divine heritage, and to reflect God's accommodating ways with humankind in its own theology and art.

3. Contextualization can give new meaning to gospel proclamation and occasion a fresh hearing of it for a particular people.

We began this theological discussion with the assertion that greater contextuality in preaching can assist the pastor in removing false stumbling blocks to the hearing of the gospel. As the pastor becomes more aware of congregational subcultures, she or he also becomes more aware of the ways in which the theology and art of the sermon can prohibit a genuine hearing of the gospel message.

Yet it is also the case that contextualism in preaching serves an equally significant proactive function. Namely, it affords the opportunity for biblical text and contemporary experience to be wedded in such a way that a new and fresh hearing of the gospel message is occasioned and new meaning is given birth.

Old Testament scholar Walter Brueggemann speaks of this reality when he writes:

> The sermon is not an act of reporting on an old text, but it is an act of making a new text visible and available. This new text in part is the

old text, and in part is the imaginative construction of the preacher which did not exist until the moment of utterance by the preacher. Like a conductor "rendering" Beethoven so that the particular music exists only in that occasion, so the preacher renders a text so that it only exists in that particular form in that particular occasion of speaking.[18]

Preaching, then, has to do with the construction of meaning. Its meaning is not "invented" or created *ex nihilo.* Rather, meaning in preaching is forged in a metaphorical way as two things which had not previously been placed side-by-side—namely a particular biblical text (or texts) and a particular congregational context—are allowed to live together and talk together and dance with one another in the imagination of the preacher, until something new occurs through their encounter.

How dull and boring our work would be if we were only reporting, over and over again, on an old text! But how exciting the task of the preacher becomes when we discover that, when wedded with new and ever-changing contexts, old texts reveal new and surprising meanings. A renewed focus upon congregations and their subcultures can assist the preacher in the creative task of meaning-making.

Preaching as "Local Theology"

Congregational Christian preaching is then, at its best, a highly contextual act of constructing and proclaiming theology within and on behalf of a local community of faith. It requires of the preacher interpretation of biblical texts, interpretation of contemporary contexts (including congregations and their subcultures), and the imaginative construction and communication of *local theology* that weds the two in a fitting and transformative way.

I borrow the term "local theology" from missiologist Robert Schreiter, who uses it to refer to theologies on the global scene which are highly contextual in nature—taking as their starting point the analysis of local cultures, and stressing the development of theological understandings that are appropriate for a particular people.[18] Examples include *minjung* (people's) theology of South Korea, various Latin American theologies of liberation, and indigenous theologies of diverse cultural groups within the United States (such as African American, feminist, or Native American theologies).

While "local theology" can be used in such a "macro" sense, we are suggesting that the term can also be used appropriately in a "micro" sense to refer to sermons shaped in and for very particular congregational subcultures within the United States. Each time the preacher sits in her study, preparing a sermon for her congregation, she is crafting local theology—theology that not only takes seriously larger church traditions, but that also attends with equal seriousness to the worldview, life experiences, and prior traditions of her own very particular congregation.

We have long recognized that preaching is, at its heart, a theological act. While exegesis of biblical texts and exegesis of congregational contexts are preaching's necessary precursors, they are not its end goal. The preacher as "practical theologian" must also bring the worlds of text and context together in one creative and imaginative act of theological construction we call the sermon. In preaching, then, theology is created.

We have also long recognized the significance of doctrinal and ecclesial theology for preaching. One of the primary functions of the pastor in the life of a congregation is to be a resident ecclesial theologian—a person who has been trained in church history and Christian doctrine, and who can assist the congregation in thinking theologically about their lives and the world. In preaching, as in other aspects of ministry, pastors are theologians of the larger church—insuring that local understandings of the Christian faith remain in continual dialogue with broader denominational and ecumenical understandings of the faith.

An emphasis on contextuality in preaching, however, points pastors toward another equally important reality. Congregational preachers are also *local theologians*, called to craft theology that is shaped for very particular communities of faith. Preaching in this understanding shares traits in common with theologies that emerge from base communities in Latin America.[19] It is culturally specific, responsive to local concerns, and highly attentive to its own "base community" in its formulation.

One of the commentators on an early draft of the *Handbook for Congregational Studies* emphasized the potential linkages between congregational theologizing in the United States and contextual liberation theologies of the two-thirds world when he wrote: "The real promise of Congregational Studies in the context of the American church is that it may become a means of *indigenizing our theological heritage in the first world in the way that base communities are doing in the third world.*"[20]

Rather than importing theologies of other cultures whole cloth into our preaching and trying to force a fit between patterns that have emerged within a different culture and our own, preaching as local theology insists that we begin with a searching examination of our own culture.

We turn now to a fuller exploration of some of the implications for preaching when it is viewed not solely as practical or ecclesial theology, but also as an intentionally "local" articulation of the Christian faith.

Hallmarks of Preaching as Local Theology

To conceive of preaching as *local* theology is to reconfigure some of the ways in which we think about the homiletical task. What occurs is not so much an overthrow of old homiletical values (excellence in biblical exegesis, theological coherence and depth, clarity, and creativity in sermon design, appropriate use of image, story, and metaphor) as it is a change in perspective. Rather than looking at preaching from "above"—from the pulpit or the scholar's study, we begin to consider it from "below"—from its inception, birthing, and hearing in the midst of congregational life.

What are the hallmarks of preaching as *local* theology? Let us briefly consider six of its underlying assumptions and aspirations.

*1. Preaching as **local** theology celebrates week-to-week congregational preaching, and the power of the particular in gospel proclamation.*

Lutheran pastor Edmund Steimle once said, "the timeless sermon, the sermon which could be preached a hundred years ago as well as today, is a poor sermon. . . . if sermons are to be biblical in the deepest sense, they will convey the truth in terms of the now. They will be secular, of this age, in every respect."[21] Preaching as local theology shares Steimle's bias against generic sermons and celebrates sermons that are written for a particular congregation of people in a particular time and place.

As a preaching professor I am sometimes asked, "Who do you think are the greatest preachers on the American scene today?" My difficulty in answering that question is that I genuinely believe the greatest preachers today are ones whose names are probably not well known outside a radius of a few miles: local pastors who week-in and week-out faithfully bring the gospel and contemporary life together in ways that capture the imaginations, deepen the faith, and stretch the vision of local faith communities. Fred Craddock echoes this sentiment when he writes:

> Much hoopla to the contrary, the most effective preachers in this or any generation are pastors, whose names we may or may not ever know. This is not a comment on oratorical skills nor is it a broad benediction on every pulpit effort by pastors. *It is rather a recognition of the central importance of knowing one's hearers, a fact which makes it possible for the sermon to have that irreplaceable source of power: appropriateness.*[22]

Preaching as local theology values the local and particular in proclamation, and encourages the preparation of sermons that are *not* easily portable from one parish to the next. Indeed, when preaching is viewed as local theology, the proverbial sermon "barrel" is helpful only as far as the universals of human experience will carry it. Otherwise, what tasted like good wine in one congregation may well taste like decaying grapes in the next.

*2. Preaching as **local** theology is not only proclaimed "to" but also "out of the midst" and "on behalf of" a local faith community.*

Preaching is not only a conversation between human beings. It is also an act of worship, an offering of praise and adoration that the pastor makes on behalf of the congregation with God as audience. In preaching the pastor not only speaks to the congregation on behalf of God. The pastor, as representative of the gathered faith community, also speaks before God on behalf of the people, giving witness to the faith they corporately share.

Fred Craddock says that "sermons should speak *for* as well as *to* the congregation. The Bible is the church's book, not the minister's alone, and therefore a proclamation of its affirmations is the church's word to itself and to the world."[23] Thus, Craddock urges preachers to proclaim the gospel in such a manner that it elicits the "nod of recognition" from those in their congregation, so that "the listeners say, 'Yes, that is my message, that is what I have wanted to say.'"[24]

When preaching is viewed as local theology, the pastor is reminded that she or he is not the sole "resident theologian" in the local community of faith; rather she or he is one of many resident theologians who contribute to the questions, insights, struggles, and life situations which feed the formation of the Sunday sermon. Instead of viewing preaching as an act in which theologically educated pastors help uneducated lay people attain unto their level of knowledge and expertise, preaching as local theology calls us to view our task with greater humility—respecting and affirming the wealth of theological knowledge and wisdom already present within the congregation, and the many ways in which congregations shape and feed the theology which finds its voice in the pulpit.

M. M. Thomas of India, a renowned ecumenist and lay theologian, gave an address almost half a century ago (in 1950) to the World Student Christian Federation in which he claimed that "living" theology is theology that is undertaken by lay persons as they seek to hear and obey God in the midst of their secular jobs.

> Theology is the *kerygma* of the Gospel made intelligible. In this sense theology is "the cutting line" between the Word and the world. It is the Word confronting the world. Therefore, the life and activity of the lay [person] seeking to hear and obey the Word of God in the day-to-day decisions of the secular job is the stuff of living theology.[25]

Preaching as local theology recognizes with Thomas that a part of the pastor's calling is "the task of making explicit what the Christian lay[person], through his [or her] confrontation with the world, knows to be the contemporary Word of God, but . . . cannot properly articulate in theological language." The pastor carefully listens to laypersons as they "in their non-theological language utter the Word of God that has come to them in their life and work in the world."[26]

Much preaching in our day suffers from an "over-againstness" in which the preacher mounts the pulpit to cajole, correct, challenge, instruct, or in some other manner "shape up" the congregation. Preaching as local theology calls upon pastors to reclaim a renewed sense of "with-ness"—moving to the pulpit out of the midst of the congregation to give witness to the congregation's own deepest beliefs, doubts, questions, longings, and fears, while also standing with the congregation before a God who confronts and challenges us all.

3. Preaching as local theology seeks to be "seriously imaginable" within a local community of faith.

In his book *The Uses of Scripture in Recent Theology* theologian David Kelsey recommends three yardsticks by which to judge the adequacy of any theological construction.[27] First, the theology must be a reasoned form of discourse, capable of consistent formulation and argued defense. Second, the theology must be faithful to the structure of Christian tradition—collapsing neither the "over againstness" of God in relation to the community nor stressing the present, particular situation at the expense of its grounding in Jesus Christ. Finally, the theology must be *seriously imaginable* to a particular people in a particular time and place. The term "seriously imaginable" involves possibilities that are both "real"—as opposed to mere fantasy—and "for *us*"—that is, imaginable within the particular social world a people inhabit.

While preaching is not systematic theology (the primary concern in Kelsey's work), it is a theological act in which the preacher is also accountable to the larger community of faith. Thus preaching, too, should meet Kelsey's criteria for theological adequacy. The theology expressed in our sermons should be intelligible and capable of reasoned defense, grounded in Scripture and church tradition, and "seriously imaginable" for culturally conditioned people. Like a three-legged stool, preaching teeters precariously if any one of these foundations is neglected.

While all three standards are critical for faithful proclamation, however, it is the third criterion—of being seriously imaginable—that is of particular import for the contextual preacher. When Kelsey discusses this criterion, he assumes that theologians and their audiences share a culture (broadly defined) that places some limits on the shaping of theology. Theologians are thereby constrained to theological articulation that can be imagined as a real possibility for shaping the personal and community identity of a particular people.[28] It is not enough to speak of the presence of God and the forms of life appropriate in God's presence in terms that can be imagined in fantasy, yet cannot be envisioned as real possibilities for real people in their real social worlds. Theology should be formed in such a way that people from out of the midst of their own sociocultural location can affirm, "Yes, we can envision that as a real possibility for us."

Since cultures are ever in flux, Kelsey acknowledges that what is "seriously imaginable" is also in flux. Theology constructed in one culture or era may lose its force in another. For example, of B. B. Warfield's late nineteenth-century ideational mode of speaking of God's presence in the world, Kelsey writes:

> The passage of time has not so much disproved him as made him seem terribly culture-conditioned. And to insist that a Christian community now adopt his hypothesis might seem a demand that it archaize itself into a culture now gone, much as though it were being required to adopt pre-Copernical [humanity's] attitudes toward the heavens.[29]

Kelsey admits that there is a liability in placing cultural constraints on theology. Theologians may find themselves simply reformulating that which is already imagined in a culture, and theology will lose its distinctive Christian witness. Yet he also contends that theology has no choice but to take such risks. The theologian must engage his or her imagination toward the construction of "seriously imaginable" theology for a particular people in a particular time and place.

> Only by an imaginative act can theological proposals capable of capturing the imaginations of real [people] living in a particular culture be concrete enough to be really "practical" for particular [people] and significantly "critical" of particular Christian communities. Only because it is grounded in a decisive imaginative act is a set of theological proposals really incarnate in [people's] real lives."[30]

Preaching, like any theological form, must run the risk of being constrained by culture in order that it can speak an incarnate "practical" and "critical" biblical word to and for culture. Yet it is precisely at the juncture of becoming seriously imaginable that the diverse subcultural worlds of preaching make its task more complicated. A sermon that is seriously imaginable in one congregation may not be as readily imaginable in another subculturally different congregation. Similarly, proclamation that the preacher deems seriously imaginable will not always be as readily imaginable for his or her congregation. (Witness, for example, the Christ as "sun" sermon with which we began this chapter.)

Preaching as local theology calls pastors to a deeper probing of congregations and their cultures so that they are enabled to prepare more seriously imaginable sermons. By exegeting the local congregation and its own particular world of meaning and value, the pastor gains clues for the shaping of sermons which cause the congregation to respond, "Yes, we can imagine the world conveyed through that sermon as a real possibility for us."

4. Preaching as **local** *theology is a "hearer-oriented" event.*

Some missiologists have suggested that we approach communication across cultures as being either "hearer-oriented" or "speaker-oriented."[31] Although the terms posit a polarity that doesn't often exist in a pristine form in human communication (since most communication employs both forms, or resides somewhere on a continuum between the two), they still provide a useful framework for thinking about communication within the preaching event.

In speaker-oriented communication, primary emphasis is placed upon the speaker's ability to communicate the message accurately and correctly. The goal is that the information reach the hearer without any adulteration or change. The speaker encodes the message in language and symbols familiar to the speaker, and may choose to do so in a very esoteric way. What is most important is that none of the essential content be lost in transmission of the message. If there are any adjustments to be made in understanding in this communication mode, they are to be made by the hearer. It is the hearer's responsibility to adapt to the speaker's communicational framework in order to comprehend the meanings communicated through the message.

An example of speaker-oriented pedagogy was my own memorization of the *Westminster Shorter Catechism* as a child. The goal in this process was not that the theological concepts contained in the questions and answers of the catechism be translated into my childish vernacular or even that I be able to paraphrase their essence in my own words. Rather, the goal was that I be able to repeat the (often unintelligible to me) words of the catechism—verbatim and without change—just as I had committed them to memory. Although I did not fully understand the meaning of the words as I learned them, the hope was that I would grow into fuller understanding of them as I matured (in the same way that children commit poetry, Scripture, or liturgical texts to memory and grow into fuller understanding of their meaning throughout their lives).

In hearer-oriented communication, on the other hand, primary value is placed upon the ability of the hearer to understand the message in his or her own symbolic framework, and to relate it to his or her own world. The speaker varies the language and symbols used in communication in order to achieve maximum understanding and appropriation by the hearer, even if some peripheral aspects of the content are lost or altered in transmission. The speaker's concern for control of the message and detailed accuracy is less important than the hearer's ability to understand and appropriate the essential meaning of the message within his or her own vernacular. Thus, the speaker seeks, as much as possible, to enter into the hearer's own world of symbolic understanding in the communication of the message.

Preaching as local theology stresses the preacher's responsibility to prepare sermons that are hearer-oriented—sermons in which preacher meets congregants on their ground, rather than requiring congregants to meet preacher on his or her ground. Reflecting the image of the God who (as Calvin reminds us) accommodated Godself to us in order to enter our frame of reference and aid our understanding, the preacher lets go some of his or her own communicational prerogatives in order to proclaim from within the congregation's own symbolic framework, the transformative message of the gospel.

*5. Preaching as **local** theology has as a goal the transformation of the imaginations of the hearers in accordance with the message of the gospel.*
Long ago Augustine, author of the first major homiletical textbook for Christian preachers, said that preaching should strive "to teach, to delight and to persuade" in order that the gospel be heard "intelligibly, willingly and obediently."[32] His goals for proclamation—incorporating educational, communicational, and persuasional elements—are still worthy goals for holistic preaching today.

More recently theologian Garrett Green has suggested that the formal capacity in human beings through which thinking, delighting, and persuading are integrated is in the human imagination. Imagination, in Green's understanding, is not the opposite of reality but rather "the means by which manifold forms of both reality and illusion are mediated to us."[33] Its biblical correlate is the "heart," which, like the imagination, functions as the seat both of intellect and emotion.[34] Rather than being a particular human faculty per se, the imagination serves an integrative function, bringing together in human experience various human abilities and potentials.

Green revisits the Barth-Brunner debate over natural theology (the debate in which Brunner claimed there was some remnant of the divine left in us human beings that enabled us to apprehend God, and in which Barth responded with a hearty *Nein!*) and contends that the imagination is the formal locus through which God's revelation to us human beings is mediated. To be created in the image of God is to have the capacity to imagine God rightly—a capacity that has been completely distorted in human beings by sin. While human beings still have the formal ability to imagine, they have lost the ability to imagine God rightly, and thus cannot enter into a right relationship with God. It is only through faith in Jesus Christ—the full image of the invisible God—that the idolatrous imaginations of human beings can be transformed and right relationships with God and neighbor restored.

Because Green views the imagination as the integrative capacity through which God's revelation to human beings is mediated, the significance of imagination for preaching becomes critical. He defines preaching as "an appeal to the imagination of the hearers through the images of scripture,"[35] and says the preacher's primary task is to employ his or her own imagination in the task of mediating and facilitating the link between Scripture and congregation. In a startling and provocative statement Green declares, "*To save sinners, God seizes them by the imagination. . . .*"[36]

Preaching as local theology trusts in God's ability to seize the imaginations of sinners through proclamation, and encourages the local pastor to place his or her own theological imagination in service to God's salvific work. However, if the preacher is going to re-image the world of the congregation according to the paradigms of Scripture, she or he must first have some grasp of the imaginative patterns concerning God, humanity, nature, and their interrelationships that are already operative in congregational life. At what junctures is the imagination of the congregation true and in accordance with the patterns revealed in Scripture, and at what junctures is it false and in need of correction? Where is congregational imagination balanced (holding together tensions that co-exist in Scripture itself), and where is it unbalanced? It is to that sixth and final hallmark of preaching as "local theology"—the necessity for congregational exegesis—that we now turn our attention.

6. In preaching as local theology, exegesis of the congregation and its subcultures is not peripheral to proclamation, but central to its concerns.
If the preacher is to strive toward proclamation which (1) celebrates the local and particular, (2) arises out of the midst of and is spoken on behalf of a local faith community, (3) is seriously imaginable, (4) is hearer-oriented, and (5) is capable of transforming congregational imagination, then it is imperative that the preacher first listen attentively to the congregation itself. It is impossible to address particular local issues and concerns unless one has first discerned what the cutting-edge issues are in congregational life. It is impossible to speak "on behalf of people" unless one has first discerned what it is that they actually believe. It is impossible to preach in a more "seriously imaginable" way unless one first has some idea of the imaginative worlds congregants already inhabit. It is impossible to shape proclamation in a more "hearer-oriented" direction unless one first becomes acquainted with the vocabulary, symbols, and thought forms which are common to a congregation's corporate life. And it is impossible to preach in a way that transforms the imaginations of the hearers in accordance with the gospel, unless one first becomes acquainted with the imaginative paradigms that are deemed to be normative in congregational life, and the junctures at which the gospel would affirm, challenge, stretch, or invert them.

When preaching is conceived as local theology, exegesis of the congregation and its subcultures is critical for every aspect of the sermon preparation task: from the selection of appropriate biblical texts for proclamation, to the questions the pastor takes to texts on behalf of the congregation, to the hermeneutical linkages forged between congregation and text, to the language, illustrations, and communicational design of the sermon. Nothing in the theology or art of the sermon falls outside the rubric of "local."

In the next chapter we will propose a method by which preachers, like cultural anthropologists, can exegete the signs and symbols of congregational culture and deepen their understanding of the imaginative worlds congregants inhabit. But first let us pause to consider some of the roles played by the pastor when preaching is conceived as local theology.

Roles of the Preacher as Local Theologian

When one surveys current missiological literature regarding "contextualization" of the gospel on the global scene, it becomes apparent that there is significant disagreement regarding to whom the task of contextualization properly belongs. Missiologist Louis Luzbetak, for example, asserts that "the only really meaningful contextualizers are the members of the local Christian community."[37] The task of constructing a local theology rightly belongs to indigenous participants in a local faith community and is undertaken only in a very limited way by those who are outsiders to that community.

Charles Kraft, on the other hand, outlines an extensive theological methodology for expatriate missionaries in his book *Communicating Christ Cross-Culturally.* When Kraft speaks of "contextualization," he is primarily referring to the intercultural communication of the gospel by missionaries in forms and modes appropriate to new cultural contexts. Kraft clearly believes that outsiders to a culture can play a significant role in the contextual task.

The differences in perspective articulated by these two missiologists cause us to raise certain questions regarding the role of the local pastor/preacher in contextualization. First, is the pastor to be considered an "insider" or an "outsider" to congregational culture in the construction of local theology (and of what significance is the pastor's perspective for contextualization in preaching)? Second, what is the relationship between the role of the congregation and the role of the pastor in the shaping of preaching as local theology? Can we, with Kraft, assert that local theology can be shaped effectively by pastors who are relative newcomers to a community of faith? Or does genuinely local theology only find its voice through those who are indigenous to or long-term residents of a local congregation?

In order to explore both sets of questions, we turn now to a fuller examination of the local pastor's stance and roles when preaching is viewed as the construction of local theology.

Insider/Outsider

Our observations in chapter 1 regarding the subcultural differences that exist among pastors and their congregations would indicate that pastors are often compelled to function in a dual role in congregational life—both as "insiders" (those who, to a certain extent, become acculturated into the idiom and life of a particular local congregation and its subculture) and as "outsiders" (those whose acting and speaking also reflect worldviews and values that are different from those held by members of the local congregation). The longer a pastor serves a congregation and becomes acculturated into its ways, the more of an insider she or he is likely to become. Yet many pastors discover that congregations, like small towns, only grant true insider status to those who were born into their culture—or have lived there at least fifty years!

Pastors—especially new pastors—can find the tension disconcerting. On the one hand, they are immediately welcomed and afforded a place of belonging within the life of the congregation and its structures. On the other hand, they are also warned (by other pastors and peers) about the dangers involved if they ever completely settle in and become too much "at home" in congregational life. ("Don't look within the congregation to find your best friends." "Take care that you don't become so comfortable with your people that you lose your 'cutting edge' in ministry." "Remember that in any social setting with congregation members you are still the 'pastor.'")

While life in this liminal state can be difficult for the pastor (and the pastor's family), the truth is that both insiders and outsiders have significant contributions to make to the construction of local theology. The pastor's dual status can actually be a significant asset for contextual preaching.

As *insider* the pastor not only becomes personally immersed in the interior life of a congregation—its idiom, customs, and history. The pastor is also afforded immediate access to other congregational insiders who can teach him or her about the congregation and its cultures. In almost every congregation there are long-term members who are delighted to help educate pastors by sharing their own stories about the congregation and its culture. Wise pastors listen attentively, and gain a wealth of congregational knowledge in this way.

Insider status also allows the preacher greater opportunity for identification with the congregation in proclamation. Walter Brueggemann says that in most church situations of biblical interpretation three voices are operative: that of the biblical text, of pastor, and of congregation. Yet all too often pastors team up with texts to

"triangle" against their congregations in preaching, leaving the congregation "a hostile, resistant outsider" who is understandably angry
to be excluded from the triangle. How much better, contends
Brueggemann, if the pastor stands with the congregation against the
text, letting the radical Word of God offend both![38] For pastors who
are willing to adopt Brueggemann's strategy, an ability to identify
with the congregation, to use "insider" descriptions that elicit from
the congregation the response, "Yes, that is who we are," is not
optional, it is essential.

Finally, insider status affords the preacher the right both to celebrate the best of congregational culture, and the right to criticize its
weaknesses. As insider the preacher can remind people of times in
their own history and common life when they have been faithful to
the gospel. And as insider—one who has stood with a congregation
in good times and bad, one who has been pastor as well as prophet—
the preacher earns the right to be heard when speaking hard truths
in love.

However, there are also liabilities that come when local theologies
are solely constructed by insiders. Robert Schreiter, a Roman Catholic theologian who has attended a great deal to the construction of
local theologies on the global scene, helpfully reminds us that "root-
edness in a community . . . does not in itself guarantee theological
insight."[39] Indeed, it may breed theological myopia. Therefore local
theologies are also in need of the perspectives "outsiders" bring to
their formulation.

One of the gifts of the *outsider* is the ability to perceive things taking place in a local culture that long-term locals may not be able to
see. Because of their fresh apprehension of a culture and their experience in other cultures, outsiders can often identify patterns or trends
that insiders to a culture are too close to perceive. Just as one cannot
discern the shape of letters on a page if the book is held too close to
the face, so the reader of a culture cannot always perceive the distinctive shape and contours of a culture in which she or he is daily
immersed.

According to Schreiter, outsiders also tend to adopt a more analytical and explanatory approach to cultural understanding than insiders. They not only seek to understand the culture; they also try to
translate their understanding into symbols that have meaning

beyond the local culture itself.[40] While insiders frequently describe their cultural experiences in narrative form, using an "idiom" familiar to other insiders, outsiders are able to translate their understandings of the culture into categories and frameworks that have meaning beyond the local culture.

The preacher as outsider, then, brings essential gifts to the task of constructing local theology in the congregational context. As outsider, the preacher is able to provide categories through which those within and those without the congregation can deepen their understanding of the congregation and its subcultures. Such descriptions can provide the transition to a new way of acting and being.

(For example, many denominational bodies do not understand why small congregations, located near one another geographically and strapped financially, don't merge and become one larger congregation. The congregations themselves are often strongly resistant to such mergers, yet are not always able to articulate their own deepest reasons for resistance. The pastor as "outsider" can serve a dual role—deepening the local congregation's awareness of its own unique identity and ways in which that uniqueness might influence a merger decision, while at the same time educating larger ecclesial bodies regarding congregational differences and their potential effect upon merger discussions.)

As outsider, the preacher can also be made more acutely aware of those significant junctures in congregational life at which a transformative gospel word needs to be spoken. Sometimes it takes the perspective of an outsider to help insiders see that ways of operating they perceive to be warm, friendly, and embracing are actually perceived by those outside the community as being exclusive, prejudiced, or inhospitable. Or, on the other hand, sometimes it takes the perspective of an outsider to help discouraged insiders see a new and hopeful vision for their future.

Finally, if it is insider status that affords a preacher the right to be heard when speaking tough truths, it is outsider status which affords both the freedom and the imperative to speak those truths. In preaching the gathered community is confronted by the God who not only dwells in our midst, but who also comes to us from beyond—speaking to us out of depths of mystery and wonder we cannot begin to fathom, calling us to lives of faithfulness we have not yet begun to grasp. It is this God—God the stranger, the outsider—to whom the preacher also gives witness in proclamation.

The contextual preacher's stance, then, is necessarily awkward and uncomfortable. With one foot firmly planted in the congregation, and one foot firmly planted in a larger Gospel vision, the preacher straddles the abyss—striving to love and affirm the congregation, while, at the same time, prodding and stretching it toward a larger worldview and greater faithfulness to its own gospel. Out of such awkward grace, transformative proclamation is given birth.

Prophet, Poet, and Theologian

The issues raised by missiologists at the outset of our discussion pose a more fundamental question for preaching, however. Namely, is the pastor the appropriate person to be proclaiming local theology in the first place? Or (as Luzbetak suggests) is local theology only appropriately shaped by those who are indigenous to the faith community—those lay members of the congregation who have been a part of its life and witness for many years?

Certainly our discussion thus far would indicate that preaching as local theology is not constructed Lone Ranger style. It is always crafted in community. The pastor who is seeking to proclaim the gospel in a "local" style will always have an ear to the community—listening for the questions, the concerns, the struggles, the issues of faith that need to be addressed in congregational life, and seeking from the community some indication as to which solutions are also genuine, authentic, and seriously imaginable within their own experience.

In a sense, then, when preaching is viewed as local theology, the true "resident theologian" is deemed to be the congregation itself. However, to make such a claim is not to imply that everything the congregation does or says can be regarded as "theology." Nor is it to suggest that preaching should return to the preacher-on-a-barstool congregational gabfests of the sixties. (Indeed, when theology and preaching are reduced to "whatever anyone chooses to contribute," both can be seriously diminished.) Rather, such a statement affirms the corporate nature of the preaching event, and highlights the significant role the congregation can and should play in the shaping of theology for proclamation.

Robert Schreiter draws a helpful distinction between the roles played by the community and by certain individuals in the construction of local theologies.[41] Schreiter affirms that the experience of the whole local community of faith is indispensable both for the formation of local theology and for its acceptance. The community, in a broad sense, is the "author" of local theology. Out of the local community arise many of the questions theology must address, the experience of having lived and wrestled with those questions and struggled with different answers, and the recognition as to which solutions make sense in light of their experience.

However, not everything the local community of faith does or says can be termed "theology." Nor does the community as a whole actually shape theology in verbal or symbolic form. Rather, there are gifted individuals within the community—poets, prophets, and professional theologians—who give actual shape and voice to local theology which, in turn, is either accepted or rejected by the community. *Prophets* serve to initiate new theological thinking by passing judgment on theology previously accepted or developed by the community. *Poets*, through symbol and metaphor, give artful expression to a local community's experience of Christian faith. *Professional theologians* help the community clarify its own experience and relate it to Scripture and traditions of the church universal. They hold the local church and the larger church in mutual accountability to one another.

While Schreiter discusses these roles as if they belong to separate and distinct individuals, faithful preaching requires of the pastor aptitude in all three roles at once! As *prophets* we are called to measure the adequacy of congregational local theologies in light of a bigger gospel, and to bring a word of judgment on all false theologies and idolatries our local communities of faith hold dear. We do so in the recognition that it is only when people have been confronted with the death of the old order and have grieved its demise that they can make way for the new (and energizing) inbreaking of God's reign.[42]

As *poets* we are called to weave the gospel and contemporary experience together anew in images and symbols that capture and transform the imaginations and hearts of our hearers. Through poetic speech we envisage in "seriously imaginable" ways the new possibilities life within God's reign affords a local community of faith.

And as *theologians* we are called not only to give voice to theologies that arise out of communal life and not only to hold our local theologies accountable to a larger church tradition, but also to see that the larger church tradition does not lose sight of the questions, insights, and challenges presented it by local faith communities.

Juggling these roles is not an easy task for the preacher. Yet if Augustine's goals for preaching (teaching, delighting, and persuading) are to be achieved, the preacher as local theologian must wear all three hats—and frequently all at the same time.

Conclusion

When preaching is viewed as "local theology" the goal is not only that proclamation strive toward greater faithfulness to the gospel of Jesus Christ as revealed in the Scriptures. The goal is also that preaching become—in its theology and its art—more fitting, seriously imaginable, and transformative for local congregations. Finding its prototypes in the preaching of Jesus, the early apostles, and countless faithful local pastors through the ages, contextual proclamation reflects the accommodating ways in which God has dealt with humanity in revelation. It requires of the pastor a willingness to let go of some of his or her own prerogatives in order to enflesh the gospel in theology, language, and forms which are accessible to and meaningful within the culture of the hearers.

Contextual preaching, then, presupposes an ever-deepening acquaintance with the congregation and its cultures. Exegesis of congregational subcultures is not peripheral, but central to its concerns. Unfortunately, however, many local pastors lack adequate training and skills in undertaking such exegesis. It is, then, to a method for local congregational exegesis that we next turn our attention, proposing in the process yet another role for the preacher—that of ethnographer.

3
Exegeting the Congregation

In his book *Widening the Horizons,* pastoral theologian Charles Gerkin proposes that practical theology is a "narrative hermeneutical" undertaking. Practical theology involves reflection upon the meanings of the biblical narrative (and its component stories, images, and themes), reflection upon the meanings of the Christian community's life and work in its various dimensions, and a "fusion of horizons" that brings the "worlds of meaning" together in a mutually critical and potentially transformative way.[1]

While postponing a more detailed discussion of "horizon fusing" for preaching until chapter 4, I do want to affirm with Gerkin that preaching—an act of constructing local practical theology—is, at its core, an interpretive (hermeneutical) enterprise. It requires of the pastor skill in interpreting the texts of Christian tradition, skill in interpreting the texts of congregational life and activity, and skill in bringing the two worlds together in seriously imaginable and transformative ways for a local community of faith.

As has already been observed, however, pastors have not always been as well trained in congregational exegesis as they have been in biblical exegesis. While many pastors would like to aim toward preaching which can be deemed "local practical theology," they are also in need of methodologies by which to plumb the depths of congregational contexts in order to come to fuller and more nuanced understandings of their subcultural assumptions.

In this chapter we will outline one approach to congregational analysis—a symbolic (or "semiotic"[2]) approach—that can assist the local preacher in discerning and interpreting the "texts" of congregational life and activity. Assuming that congregations are indeed subcultures—each with its own particular communicative network of signs and symbols—we will encourage pastors to become amateur cultural anthropologists, studying and interpreting the symbols of congregational life in order to gain greater understanding of congregational subcultural identity.

To focus primarily upon congregational identity, and to analyze it by a closer attending to congregational symbols, is not to suggest that other approaches to congregational analysis (such as those concentrating upon "program," "process," or "social context"[3]) are peripheral or unimportant for preaching. Holistic preaching requires a multifaceted exegetical method. Just as no single approach is adequate for interpreting biblical texts, so no single method is sufficient when it comes to interpreting living bodies as complex, dynamic, and multidimensional as local congregations.

However, a focus upon identity does remind us that at the heart of Christian worship is the formation and transformation of Christian identity—both individual and corporate—through the mysterious workings of the Holy Spirit. In worship we bring our assumptions about God, nature, time, and humanity into a realm where we encounter, through the "strange new world" of God's revelation, new ways of envisioning and living in relationship with God and all creation. In worship we offer our own limited worldviews and distorted values unto a God who can, through the Spirit's workings, extend our myopic vision and correct our astigmatisms. And in worship, we enter a realm in which we ourselves—through the singing of hymns, offering of prayers, and participation in various ritual acts—engage in a dance of faith that also serves as dress rehearsal for faithful and transformed living in the realm of God's reign.

Preaching, then, has to do with the formation and transformation of Christian identity—not only of individuals, but also of congregations. Yet if we as preachers are going to proclaim the gospel in ways capable of transforming congregational identity, we first need to become better acquainted with the ways in which our people already imagine God and the world. If we are going to aid in the extension of myopic vision or the correction of astigmatic values, then we must first strive to "see" God and the world as our people do. And if we are going to engage our people in ritual acts that enable them to become better dancers of the faith—both within worship and without—then we must first know where their steps are faltering and where they are most in need of dress rehearsal for the new age to come.

It is, then, toward the identification and interpretation of symbolic "texts" revelatory of congregational identity—that we now turn our attention.

A Symbolic Approach to Cultural Analysis

In his highly influential work, *The Interpretation of Cultures,* American anthropologist Clifford Geertz articulates his vision for interpretive anthropology: a study of the symbolic "webs of significance" human beings spin.[4] For Geertz, culture is not merely the patterned sum of human behaviors; nor is it an underlying and invisible power that causes human beings to act in certain ways. Rather, culture is a context, a public document whose symbolic actions can be observed, analyzed, and interpreted. By studying the signs and symbols of a culture—its ritual acts and practices, its rites of passage, its sacred stories—the student of culture can discern much about what a culture believes and values.

The method employed by the symbolic anthropologist is *ethnography.* Functioning within culture as a "participant-observer,"[5] the ethnographer goes into a culture, establishes rapport with its inhabitants, and analyzes the culture while also becoming immersed in its day-to-day activities. Through various methods (selecting informants, taking genealogies, keeping a diary) the ethnographer collects and documents significant cultural "texts" for study. However, such data gathering is never an end in itself. Rather, ethnographic research is always directed toward the greater end of *thick description*: moving beyond description of the symbol itself (which is "thin" description) to an interpretation of its meaning and message in relation to certain socially established codes and structures.

Gilbert Ryle, the British philosopher who coined the terms "thin" and "thick" description, offers a simple example by which to distinguish between them.[6] Suppose, says Ryle, three boys are observed engaging in nonverbal communication by rapidly closing and then opening their right eyelids. In "thin" description, an observer might report seeing three children, each of whom, one after the other, rapidly contracted his right eyelid. The reporter, in this instance, is simply describing the signs observed (eyelid contractions), without attributing meaning to the signs. In "thick" description, on the other hand, the observer moves beyond mere recounting of the children's actions to an examination of the meaning of those actions in relation to certain socially constructed codes of behavior. The observer, for example, might report that while the first boy simply had an involuntary eye twitch, the second—falsely assuming the first was winking at him—had winked at the first, and the third had engaged in an exaggerated parody of the wink of the second. In other words, the interpreter makes some educated judgments regarding the meaning of the signs observed, interpreting them within the assumed communicative codes of the culture.

Thick description, said Geertz, is the work of the ethnographer. The ethnographer goes into a culture, selects certain cultural events or "texts" for study, and seeks to discern—given the culture's own network of behavioral codes—what those signs mean. Such interpretations of meaning by those who are not native to a culture are always imaginative acts and are, thus, "fictions . . . in the sense that they are 'something made,' 'something fashioned'"[7] (not in the sense that they are false or unfactual). Cultural analysis inevitably involves a great deal of guesswork on the part of the ethnographer. Yet it is Geertz's contention that through a close analysis of very microscopic and homely events and actions within a local culture, the anthropologist can gain great insight into the larger and more abstract realm of cultural worldview and values. Indeed, for Geertz, the whole point of a symbolic analysis of culture is "to aid us in gaining access to the conceptual world in which our subjects live so that we can, in some extended sense of the term, converse with them."[8]

The Pastor as Ethnographer

Certainly for pastors, who are called to preach the gospel of Jesus Christ across subcultures in "homely" local congregational contexts, the goal of "gaining access to the conceptual world in which our subjects live so that we can . . . converse with them" is a worthy one. If preachers are to achieve the theological ends of contextualization outlined in chapter 2—removing false stumbling blocks to the hearing of the gospel, reflecting in our preaching the accommodating way in which God has dealt with humanity in revelation, and occasioning in our sermons a fresh hearing of the gospel for a particular people—then it is essential that we engage in interpretive activities that not only give access to the worlds revealed in biblical texts, but that also give access to the subcultural worlds in which our congregations live.

In other words, preachers need to become amateur ethnographers—skilled in observing and in thickly describing the subcultural signs and symbols of the congregations they serve. The task of congregational exegesis is a "microscopic" one, involving attention to the very local actions and idioms of congregational life. The task is an imaginative and interpretive one, requiring pastors to guess at meanings and constantly to reassess those guesses. And the task is an open-ended one, as the quest for meaning carries pastors into the ever-deepening waters of congregational life with its shifting tides and currents.

In carrying out the task of ethnography the preacher, like the cultural anthropologist, adopts a "participant-observer" field method. Christian educator Denham Grierson, who developed a participant-observer approach to congregational studies for Australian theological students, summarizes its guidelines as follows:

1. The participant-observer shares in the activities and sentiments of the people. This involves face-to-face relationships, and direct contact with their shared life.
2. The role of the participant-observer requires both a necessary detachment and personal involvement.
3. The participant-observer is a normal part of the culture and the life of the people under observation. He or she does not come as an expert, but rather as a learner who, in order to learn, participates in the life of the people.
4. The role of the participant-observer is consistent within the congregation, so that no confusion is created by unexpected changes of behavior or alternating of roles.
5. The participant-observer has as a target a symbolic level of meaning in the life of the congregation which cannot be gained from observing external behaviour alone, as would be the case for a detached observer.[9]

Because local pastors function both as insiders and outsiders in congregational culture,[10] they stand in a unique position for participant-observation. As insiders, preachers are able to become fully immersed in the life of the congregation they are studying; as outsiders they are also able to keep some analytical distance from it. As insiders, they are allowed access to the kinds of face-to-face relationships and activities that are most revelatory of congregational worldview and values; as outsiders, they have access to interpretive frameworks that can help place what they are learning within a broader perspective. In short, their own social location within the community of faith makes them prime candidates for carrying out participant-observation.

But is it realistic to add to the pastor's already over-extended list of tasks yet one more? Is it feasible to ask the preacher to don yet another "hat" in the great juggling act called parish ministry?

My own response to these questions is twofold. First, most parish pastors I know are already engaged in congregational subcultural exegesis at some level. Whenever I sit with local pastors at continuing education events or engage them in conversation about their congregations, they inevitably start describing their congregations—and frequently congregational subcultures—in analytical terms and categories. My intent is not to add one more "hat" to the pastor's already over-crowded role wardrobe. Rather, my hope is that pastors might become more proficient, adept, and capable of thick description while wearing the hat many of them have already donned—that of congregational exegete.

Second, for the local pastor to become ethnographer does not so much require additional time as it requires *a new way of seeing and perceiving that which already happens in the ordinary course of ministry*. In the same way that the pastor trained in "family systems theory" has a construct through which to discern previously unrecognized patterns in his counseling, so the pastor trained in the symbolic analysis of culture has access to constructs that help her perceive previously unobserved sociocultural patterns in congregational life. The latest fight at the officers' board becomes an occasion for probing more deeply into current congregational values, and the meandering stories of a shut-in open new vistas for understanding congregational ethos and worldview. Donning the hat of ethnographer is not so much about taking on new responsibilities as it is about engaging in everyday ministry with new questions, new perspectives, and new tools for interpretation.

Identifying Symbols for Study: Some Guidelines

Suppose, then, we envision the congregation as a unique and foreign subculture, bound together by its own distinctive "idiom"—a network of signs and symbols through which it communicates its particular identity. And suppose we envision ourselves as cultural anthropologists, ethnographers who are seeking to exegete and thickly describe the signs and symbols of congregational life in order to better understand its unique identity. Where do we begin? Amid the myriad of verbal and nonverbal, oral and written, auditory, visual, and tactile symbols through which congregations give witness to their distinctive identities, how do we identify those that are most fertile for subcultural exegesis? How do we distinguish between symbols that have marginal cultural significance and those that anthropologists would label *culture texts*: symbols which perform significant functions within the culture or carry for the culture pivotal meaning?[11]

The following guidelines, gleaned and adapted from the insights of anthropologists and theologians who adopt a symbolic approach to the study of culture, can assist the pastor in selecting appropriate symbols for study:

1. *Seek out those symbolic "texts" that have value and meaning to the members of the congregation itself.*

One of the best ways for the pastor to begin discerning which symbols are more important than others is by questioning which symbolic texts receive the most attention in the life of the congregation itself. For example:

- What symbols (artifacts, mementos, stories, written materials) have been preserved by the congregation and are a part of its formal or informal archival memory?
- What traditions (activities, rituals, observances) are nearest and dearest to the heart of this congregation, and cannot be changed without major upheaval in congregational life?
- What symbolic texts, in past and present, have caused most controversy in congregational life? (People tend to fight over those things they care about most deeply.)
- Which stories are repeated with greatest frequency in the recounting of the congregation's own story?
- What was it, symbolically, that attracted newcomers to the life of this congregation?

Since congregations themselves frequently signal which symbols in their common life are most laden with meaning for them, the wise pastor will listen for such clues, and follow their lead.

2. Investigate symbolic texts that take a variety of forms: verbal and nonverbal, spoken and written, audible, visual, and tactile.

"Culture texts" in congregational life take a variety of forms: verbal (sermons or favorite hymns) and nonverbal (ritual acts and gestures, architecture, visual arts); spoken (stories told by older members as they recount the congregation's history) and written (a history prepared on the occasion of a church anniversary); auditory (a musical presentation), tactile (elements used for communion), and visual (the spatial arrangement of chancel furniture). The wise exegete will attend to a wide array of congregational texts, allowing them to serve as checks and balances upon one another in the exegetical process.

3. Don't shy away from symbols or configurations of symbols that are contradictory or create dissonance for the analysis of culture.

Congregations are complex and often contradictory subcultures, not given to facile or hasty labeling. Like individuals, they may perceive themselves to have one identity, only to find that others perceive them very differently. Or, they may aspire to an identity which has not yet been realized in their midst.

The wise exegete of congregational culture will not only attend to a variety of symbols and types of symbols, but will also listen closely for the dissonances, as well as the consonances, within and among them. Frequently it is by living with symbols that seem to send conflicting messages (and refusing to rush to a hasty resolution as to their meaning) that some of the deepest insights regarding congregational identity can be gleaned.

4. Don't shy away from complex texts (such as rituals or rites of passage). While being more difficult to analyze, they may also be more revelatory of the complexities of congregational meaning.

Anthropologists tell us that culture texts can be comprised of one sign (such as a flag) or of many interacting signs (such as a worship service), and that often it is the complex texts—configurations of symbols that do not break down easily for analysis—that are the most important for disclosing cultural meaning. While the exegete of culture may begin with simpler texts for analysis, she or he should also be aware that it is frequently through the more complex texts that a more complex (and more nuanced) understanding of congregational culture begins to emerge.

5. *Attend not only to texts that are disclosive of identity (worldview, ethos, values), but also to texts that are disclosive of social change.*

One of the dangers of focusing primarily upon a study of subcultural identity in congregational life (What does the congregation believe? What does it value? What is its distinctive character or ethos?) is that concerns related to social change—both within the congregation and in relation to its surroundings—can be deemphasized. However, a lessened focus on change need not occur if the student of congregational culture intentionally seeks out texts for study related *both* to identity and to social change.

Robert Schreiter says texts that are particularly disclosive of identity are likely to be found in communal celebrations.[12] Rituals associated with rites of passage (such as those surrounding birth, puberty, marriage, and death) and celebrations associated with the incorporation of new elements into a culture (the reception of new members, the adoption of a new hymnal, the commissioning of a newly established mission team) can be particularly revelatory of cultural identity.

As for social change, texts that deal with adjudication (How are conflictual decisions made? By whom? By what process?) and rituals related to healing (What is considered to constitute a threat to the health of a community, and what processes must be followed in order to restore order and balance?) are considered fertile soil.

Seven Symbols for Congregational Exegesis

In light of the above guidelines, toward which symbols should the local pastor turn in order to begin or deepen a symbolic analysis of congregational subculture? Which particular culture texts in congregational life hold most promise for enhancing the pastor's own understanding of congregational life?

Below we will discuss seven congregational symbols that are both accessible to most local pastors for their analysis and exegesis, and that also have potential to be highly disclosive of congregational identity. The list is not meant to be exhaustive, but suggestive, since exegeting a congregation is a lot like peeling an onion (or—more dynamically—like trying to pin down an amoeba). Texts lead us to other texts that lead us to other texts, and our cultural interpretations are forever being corrected and modified in light of new findings and ongoing changes in congregational life. Thus, the list of potential texts for study in congregational life is virtually endless and constantly in flux.

Further, identification as to which of the texts discussed below are *most* critical for disclosing identity will vary from congregation to congregation. Just as the exegete of Scripture may need to try a number of avenues of textual analysis before she or he discerns which approaches are most disclosive of the deeper meanings of a particular biblical text, so the exegete of congregational culture will need to approach his or her study from a diversity of angles until she or he begins to discern which ones are most revelatory of congregational meaning in his or her particular context. It is only through a trial and error process of exegeting disparate congregational symbols and comparing and contrasting the results that the local pastor can begin to discern the patterns that give shape to congregational identity.

What this list does provide is a variety of plausible starting points for symbolic analysis of culture in congregational life—seven categories of potential culture texts that are readily accessible to a variety of pastors in a diversity of congregational contexts. If examined and thickly described, these texts can assist us in moving toward our stated goal of coming to know our congregations more deeply in order that we might also preach to them in ways that are both more fitting and more transformative for who they truly are.

1. Stories and Interviews

STORIES. One of the lasting contributions of James Hopewell to the field of congregational studies is his overt recognition of that which many pastors have long known: namely, that there is a gold mine to be discovered through a careful attending to the stories people tell in congregational life.[13] Indeed, there are probably no more fruitful "texts" for analyzing congregational subculture than the narratives participants in congregational life share with the pastor in the ordinary process of carrying on ministry.

In one of the four congregations where I first served as pastor there was a long-time member named Sam who liked to accompany me on visits to newcomers and the unchurched in the community. Sam was a seventy-year-old dairy farmer who not only had a passion for evangelism—he was also a virtual repository of local lore and could entertain me and those we visited for hours by spinning yarns about events that had happened in that country church and its surrounding community. The stories Sam told ranged from the humorous (such as the tale about the snake that was drawn out of hibernation by the warmth of the church sanctuary on a cold winter's Sunday and chose to make its appearance in the middle of the sermon—poking its head through the wooden paneling just over the preacher's head!) to the serious (such as the story about the lawsuit several members of the congregation had filed on behalf of poorer members of the community in order to insure that they received fair payment when the state corporation commission condemned their land to make way for a new nuclear power plant).

Over time it began to dawn upon me that much (if not most) of what I knew about that congregation's history and heritage I had learned through Sam's stories. Taken together those individual yarns helped me piece together a larger tapestry that was disclosive of the congregation's own story. And through that larger story I discovered a great deal about that rural congregation's unique character, identity, and witness within its own context.

James Hopewell says that it is through a depth analysis of that larger congregational story—its setting, characterization, and plot—that pastors as local theologians can begin to discern the distinctive parameters of congregational worldview, ethos, and character.[14] He encourages us not only to listen intently to the stories people tell us, but also to ask certain questions in order to unearth latent meanings.

Among the questions that can be helpful to the pastor in exegeting congregational stories are the following:

- Who are identified as heroes in the stories of congregational life, and what are the qualities that have made them so? Or, who are identified as villains in this congregation's stories, and what are the characteristics that have made them so?

- Where are the silences in the storytelling of the congregation—
  the things everyone knows (or at least all the insiders), but no
  one talks about? (Are there pastors or church staff persons
  who are never mentioned in the recounting of congregational
  history? Are there secrets from the past that are whispered in
  private, but never discussed openly in congregational life?)
  What do those silences tell you about this congregation?
- Are there any recurring images or metaphors in the congregational story as people tell it that give you insight into how they
  perceive themselves and their world? (For example, do congregation members consistently talk of their inability to gather
  without "eating together"? Or, do they speak of being a "haven"
  for refugees and others who seek a safe and accepting place?)
- Is there any common dream or vision that seems to unite this
  people as they move toward their common future?
- If you were to plot the story of this congregation, like the plot
  of a novel, what would that plot line look like?

INTERVIEWS. In addition to attending more closely to the stories that
voluntarily emerge in the life of ministry, pastors can also be more
intentional about seeking out and informally interviewing key people in the life of a community and a congregation who can instruct
them regarding the church's life and ministry. Anthropologist James
Clifton reminds us that one of the strategies used by ethnographers
when they enter a new culture is to identify and interview key persons who can instruct them regarding the significant events and
symbols in a culture's present and history.

> Essentially, the relationship between an ethnographer and a key infor-
> mant is that between a student and teacher or an apprentice and a
> master. The ethnographers present themselves as novices to be social-
> ized or enculturated anew, and the informant agrees to provide sys-
> tematic instruction and guidance. . . . Developing numerous such
> relationships enables the ethnographer to participate regularly and
> meaningfully in the lives of the people studied.[15]

One of the dangers faced by ethnographers is that they may
become over-involved with too narrow a range of persons, thus fail-
ing to gain a broad enough perspective on the culture being studied.
In order to be most effective, culture interviews need to be broad-

based, inclusive of cultural sages and key leaders as well as of new-comers and marginal members of the culture.

Authors in the field of congregational studies encourage pastors to conduct interviews with parishioners for a diversity of purposes. Carroll and Hopewell recommend "guided interviews" with members who have been associated with a congregation for a shorter or longer period, in order to collect oral histories of the congregation. These stories and reminiscences are essential if the student of congregational culture is to understand the forces that have shaped and formed congregational identity. Questions that might be included in such an interview are:

- What's the news around the church now?
- What changes have you noticed about the church during the time you have been associated with it?
- What has happened that has pleased you?
- What has happened that you would like not to have occurred?
- What has happened that you would like to have been followed up in a different way?[16]

An oral history can also be compiled more collectively, by gathering a group of diverse parishioners together for an evening and corporately constructing a time line that charts significant events in the church's history in relation to concurrent events in neighborhood, region, nation, and world.[17] The recollections and anecdotes that are shared and mutually corrected on such an evening can be a tremendous aid to the thick description of current congregational life. Indeed, historian James Wind urges not only the collection, but also the preservation of oral histories, so that they can become a part of a church's ongoing archives of texts for study.[18]

The value of interviews is to be found not only in what they tell us about the past, however, but also in what they tell us about the present and anticipated future in congregational life. For example, when Carroll and Hopewell turn their attention to the assessment of congregational "character," they propose a different set of questions, largely focusing upon group boundary (What separates "us" from "not us"?) issues:

- How is this church most likely to fall apart?
- What sort of talk dampens the spirit of this church?

- What distinguishes this church from (a nearby competitor)?
- What sort of church program or project is frustrating and unproductive here?
- Think of a respected member. Without naming him or her, describe his/her characteristics.
- Think of an embarrassing member. Without naming him or her, describe his/her characteristics.
- At what points in church life do you feel closest to God?
- At what points in church life do you feel in danger of losing touch with God?[19]

Interviews, whether formal or informal, conducted with individuals or with groups, can be culture texts, disclosive of congregational identity and social change. What is important for a symbolic approach to culture is that the pastor recognize them as such, and listen with the ears of an ethnographer for the latent meanings embedded in the stories key leaders and marginal participants, long-term members and newer members, elderly members and youth, would tell.

2. Archival Materials

Another primary source for culture texts is the collection of materials a congregation produces and saves in its archives. While some congregations have more formal systems for filing and preserving archival materials than others, nearly every congregation has a box, cabinet, or file drawer that contains materials that have been deemed worthy of preservation, and that holds something of the memory of congregational life.

In his own perusal of one large, historic congregation's archives, James Wind unearthed the following materials, many of which may prove to be valuable culture texts for the symbolic analyst:

- documents related to the founding of the church (articles of incorporation, deeds to the property, congregational constitution);
- minutes of the central decision-making board and of various committees and organizations;
- financial records and fund-raising brochures;
- records of official pastoral acts (baptisms, weddings, funerals);
- official reports and statistics submitted to the denomination;

- newsletters, worship bulletins, and printed sermons;
- pictures and other "representational" materials;
- cassette tape recordings;
- artifacts no longer used in congregational life.[20]

Once again, when studied as symbols and analyzed for their "thicker" meanings, these materials can give the pastor significant insight into the continuities and discontinuities in congregational identity as it has been formed and re-formed through the years.

3. Demographics

If the outsider asks a local pastor to describe his or her congregation, the picture that is often painted initially of congregational life is a demographic one—the makeup of the congregation in regard to age, sex, race, ethnicity, social class, educational level, power, or prestige. While such statistics provide only a superficial description of what we hope to describe more thickly, they nevertheless do provide valuable information about congregational identity and how it is formed. A congregation's worldview and character are shaped by who is or who isn't included in congregational life.

Furthermore, a congregation symbolically communicates a great deal about its inner life by its corporate makeup. While what is communicated may be what "is," rather than what the members would like "to become," symbolic communication nevertheless goes on. Indeed, pastors often despair of the messages that are communicated to a young visiting family with children by a congregation whose membership is largely grey-haired, or to a racial ethnic visitor by a homogenous Anglo-Saxon congregation.

Demographics can enhance knowledge of congregational identity in a variety of ways, as is evidenced in Carroll and Hopewell's partial listing of their uses:

- To provide a profile of the congregation's typical member;
- To indicate the degree of diversity that exists in a congregation;
- To compare the congregation's presumed demographic picture with its actual one;
- To provide important clues for program development for both present and potential members;

- To assist a congregation to reflect on its given demographic identity in comparison with that which it would like to become;
- To assist judicatory officials in understanding the congregations with whom they work. . . .[21]

The congregational ethnographer will be concerned not only to collect and compile demographic statistics, but more importantly, to compare and contrast them with past statistics, with statistics in the community surrounding the church building, and with the congregation's own self-perception in order to discern what thicker meanings they may convey.

4. Architecture and Visual Arts

One of the first communicative signs that greets the visitor to a local congregation is the location and architecture of the church building. An urban church building with tall gothic spires, sandwiched between skyscrapers and located in the heart of the business and political center of a city suggests, by its very placement and design, a far different identity from that of a highly contemporary, steeple-less structure of redwood and stone found in the midst of a suburban residential neighborhood.

Sociologist Douglas Walrath has identified twelve different congregational "types," based on the sociocontextual locations of their buildings alone.[22] While one might want to quibble with his types, Walrath's underlying message—that social context shapes congregational identity, and that building location symbolically communicates something about that identity—cannot be avoided. Likewise, while James Wind warns against over-identification between church buildings and the present character of their congregations,[23] he also suggests that buildings often bespeak either past or present congregational styles, and changes in a building "may provide clues to the ways in which a congregation participated in a larger plot. . . ."[24]

To the discerning eye, it is not only location and exterior architecture that communicate, but also the design and use of internal space. What is communicated by the spatial configuration of the building? Can outsiders easily find their way around? Are any spaces in the church building "owned" by one group or off-limits to others? What priorities are communicated by the way space is assigned?

If a newcomer walked through the halls of the church, glancing in church school rooms and perusing bulletin boards, what messages would be communicated? What pulse(s) of congregational life can be taken simply by observing the decorative arrangement of church school rooms; the posters, plaques, and pictures that adorn the hall walls; the nature of fellowship space; the location and decor of staff offices?

If worship is at the heart of a Christian congregation, then special attention needs to be focused upon that place where a congregation regularly gathers as a community for worship and praise. How is the sanctuary designed and arranged, and what does that design communicate about the congregation's worship life? (Does the worship space communicate a sense of awe and reverence before God, or is it primarily designed so as to enhance and celebrate Christian community? What type of furnishings are used and how are they arranged? Is the choir located in front or on the side or in back? How high is the pulpit, and where is it located? Where are the communion table and baptismal font located? What other visible symbols are present [stained glass windows, banners, flags, plaques], and what do they communicate about congregational ethos?)

The quest, as always, is not simply descriptive, but also interpretive. What deeper meanings can be gleaned about the particular worldview, character, and ethos of this congregation by observing the art and space of that building it calls "home?"

5. Rituals

"Ritual," according to Carroll and Hopewell, "is repetitive action that has more than utilitarian significance. It is a form of nondiscursive, gestural language through which a group acts out meanings and relationships that are of enduring significance to its life."[25] While some people think of ritual as essentially conservative in nature, anthropologists Victor and Edith Turner remind us that ritual can be both reflective and generative of cultural change.

> [Ritual] is not a bastion of social conservatism whose symbols merely condense cherished cultural values. Rather it holds the generating source of culture and structure.... Performances of ritual are distinct phases in the social process whereby groups adjust to internal changes and adapt to their external environment.[26]

Rituals, then, not only provide sources for discovering what congregational identity is; they also provide opportunities to probe and explore what it is becoming.

Anthropologists have provided us with distinctions among ritual types that may be helpful to the preacher as congregational exegete. For example, Stewart Guthrie distinguishes between *calendrical rites*—rituals which have some regular performance schedule according to the calendar, and *critical rites*—rituals which are only performed occasionally.[27] In studying congregational life it is important, first of all, to identify both the calendrical and the critical rites observed by a particular congregation.

Calendrical rites can be identified by asking, By what calendar(s) does this congregation structure its ritual life (liturgical year? denominational calendar? solar cycle? agricultural cycle for crops? school year?), and what are those rituals that are regularly observed (weekly, monthly, or annually)? Annually, for example, many congregations observe the seasons and festivals of the liturgical year, ordering their common life together in ecumenical unity with other Christians. However, it is sometimes through observation of those calendrical rites that are unique to congregational life—the annual week of "special" worship services, the monthly pilgrimage to a nearby nursing home for a service of communion, or the mid-week service for healing—that the greatest clues to congregational identity emerge.

Critical rites are more episodic in nature, occurring at occasions such as births (baptisms), deaths (funerals), marriages (weddings), initiations (church membership), or illness (rites associated with healing). Which rites are emphasized and which de-emphasized can again be revelatory.

In one of the rural congregations where I was pastor, infant baptisms were very rare because the church was aging and small. Thus, it became the practice of the women of that congregation to celebrate each occasion of infant baptism by purchasing a potted plant in honor of the child, placing it on the communion table during the baptismal service, and then planting it in the church yard after the baptism. That symbolic act was actually indicative of much that was highly valued in the life of that congregation: children, the earth and its fruits, and the ongoing succession of generations in that place. By contrast, when my husband and I moved to our next congregation—a young, suburban, nontraditional church with many children and a longing for more of the wisdom and experience that comes with age—a very different critical rite was observed. The entire congregation threw a party to honor its oldest member's eightieth birthday.

Anthropologist Marvin Harris provides another means by which local pastors can distinguish between various ritual acts in the church, as he draws a contrast between "rites of solidarity" and "rites of passage." In *rites of solidarity*, says Harris, participation in a ritual act "enhances the sense of group identity, coordinates the actions of individual members of the group, and prepares the group for immediate or future cooperative action."[28] Rites of solidarity serve a cohesive function within a community, intensifying its common commitments and values. *Rites of passage*, in contrast, "celebrate the social movement of individuals into and out of groups or into and out of statuses of critical importance to the community."[29] Rites of passage allow the community to publicly mark significant changes that occur in the lives of individuals and in their relationship to the community.

In congregational life, the same event sometimes functions both as a rite of solidarity and as a rite of passage. For example, a celebration of infant baptism is, on the one hand, a rite of passage, signifying a new relationship between the child, his or her parents, and the Christian community. On the other hand, an infant baptism also serves as a rite of solidarity, calling upon the gathered community to affirm its own trinitarian faith and belief, to reaffirm its own baptismal identity.

Other events can be more strongly identified with one or the other function. Homecoming and anniversary celebrations, observances of the Lord's Supper, and the commissioning of church mission teams frequently serve to reinforce congregational solidarity, while funerals, marriages, confirmations, and services of ordination often note significant rites of passage.

What is important for the congregational ethnographer is first to identify the significant rites and rituals in congregational life (be they calendrical or critical, rites of solidarity or rites of passage) and then to describe them "thickly." Such description should attend both to the ritual in all its "dramatic unity" (focusing upon the overall movement, flow, mood, and internal unity of the ritual as a whole) and to the discrete "ritual symbols" of which it is comprised (focusing upon the smaller objects, activities, relationships, words, gestures, or spatial arrangements that constitute the ritual act).[30]

6. Events and Activities

According to Clifford Geertz, the best interpretations of cultures are not achieved by "arranging abstracted entities into unified patterns" but by closely observing and interpreting local cultural *events*.[31] Indeed, the foci for Geertz's own thickly descriptive studies of culture are events: a Javanese funeral, for example, or a Balinese cockfight.

Theoretically, any event in congregational life has the potential to become a "culture text"—particularly those activities that hold special meaning and value for members of that congregation. And, once again, the pastor is wise to look both at the plethora of activities that occur on a regular basis in the life of the church (educational, missional, fellowship), as well as toward a more intensive analysis of some of them.

In compiling and assessing a catalog of congregational activities, the pastor might ask questions such as:

- Which types of activities/events receive the most attention, time, energy, and investment of resources (personal and financial) in congregational life? Which types of activities are, comparatively speaking, more neglected?
- Which activities/events in congregational life are the most controversial?
- Of which activities/events in congregational life do local church members speak with greatest pride?
- Which activities/events in congregational life have been added in recent years, and what do they suggest about the direction in which the church is currently headed? Which activities/ events have been omitted or de-emphasized in recent years, and what do they suggest about the congregation's present and future direction?
- Which activities/events distinguish this congregation from others in its surrounding environment?

Through the above screening process the student of congregational culture can begin not only to draw some general conclusions about congregational character and values, but also to identify several activities/events of congregational life that warrant more particular and focused attention as culture texts.

7. People

Finally, people themselves can be valuable culture texts, worthy of thick description. In nearly every congregation there are respected figures who, in their very beings, symbolically personify the ideals of that congregation. Although they may not be the most outspoken participants in congregational life, when they do speak, their voices are heeded because they are perceived by others to have that elusive quality called "wisdom." These admired symbols of congregational identity are frequently called upon to play major leadership roles in congregational life, and are capable of bringing healing and wholeness in times of adversity and strife. By observing these sages, a student of congregational culture can learn much about what a congregation values.

Alternatively, there also exist in congregational life people who live "on the margins"—individuals who are considered to be eccentric or extreme by other members, or who themselves will testify that they don't "fit in" (in terms of their lifestyle, beliefs, or values) as well as others. If attending to the sages can tell a pastor what is valued in a congregation, attending to those on the margins can give a signal as to where the cultural boundary lines lie that separate "us" from "not-us."[32]

A pastor recently told me that her congregation had lost several members who were fairly conservative in their theological orientation and who became increasingly frustrated with the pastor and the congregation for not holding to a conservative party line on certain social issues. The pastor commented, "You know, ours is a very open and accepting congregation. In fact, it seems to me the only thing we cannot tolerate is intolerance. When people come into our midst who insist that there is only one way to view an issue as a Christian, and start suggesting that the other members who disagree with them are not true Christians, that's when our members get up in arms. Those are the folk who have the hardest time finding acceptance and feeling at home in the life of our congregation."

The pastor's comments are revelatory regarding the values this particular congregation holds dear, and the lines that separate those in the mainstream from those on the margins of congregational culture. One can readily imagine that in another congregational subculture the same shoes might well have been on opposite feet—with those who insisted on openness on such issues being marginalized and feeling out of sync with the larger body.

Components of Cultural Identity: Worldview, Values, and Ethos

If identifying and collecting appropriate symbolic texts for study is the first step in congregational cultural analysis, the second step is an analytical and interpretive one. The ethnographer examines and analyzes the texts, seeking to deepen his or her understanding of their meaning within their own particular web of symbolic communication.

Yet the exegete of congregational culture might well ask, What is it that we are looking for? What are the components that constitute "subcultural identity" and mark its distinctiveness from another?

When anthropologists talk about cultures and their distinguishing characteristics, they use categories such as "worldview," "values," and "ethos" to assist in their comparative analyses. *Worldview* refers to a people's "picture of the way things in sheer actuality are"[33]—what they perceive to be "really real." *Values* reflect a people's interests and preferences within that world—that is, what they deem to be desirable and valuable. *Ethos* refers to "the tone, character and quality of their life, its moral and aesthetic style and mood; . . . the underlying attitude toward themselves and their world that life reflects."[34]

Anthropologists readily admit that the lines among these three characteristics are often fuzzy. An analysis of a culture's ethos necessarily involves a discussion of its values, and worldview descriptions frequently move beyond what "is" to embrace elements of the "ought." Consequently many cultural analysts use "worldview" as an umbrella term, signifying an amalgam of cultural understandings related to identity.

While recognizing the term's more comprehensive usage, Robert Redfield was one of the first anthropologists to define, in a more precise way, "worldview" and its component parts. Worldview, he said, "is the way we see ourselves in relation to all else. Every worldview is a stage set."[35] In order to assess worldview the anthropologist asks two basic questions: (1) "When this people look out from themselves to confront something else, what is it that they confront?" and (2) "What is the relation they see between themselves and that which is confronted?"[36]

By surveying studies undertaken at Yale University of several hundred societies, Redfield concluded that every worldview of every culture included beliefs and understandings regarding three primary areas and their interrelationships:

1. human nature and human societal groupings;
2. the nonhuman world (earth and sky and so forth) including spatial and temporal orientations; and
3. the supernatural world (including gods and other powerful beings or forces).

Worldview, he concluded, can be conceived as a triangle—God, nature, humanity—with their various interrelationships.[37]

Other anthropologists, recognizing and accommodating to the fuzziness among categories such as "worldview" and "values," have opted to hold the two together under a single rubric. Florence Kluckhohn and Fred Strodtbeck, for example, use the term "value-orientations"[38] not only to refer to what "is" according to a particular worldview, but also to indicate the culture's own tendencies or directionalities in regard to a particular area. They propose five different categories of value-orientations by which a student of culture can categorize his or her findings:

Human nature orientation. Are human beings perceived by the cultural grouping to be basically evil, basically good, or a mixture of good and evil? Is human nature conceived to be mutable or immutable?

Nature/supernature orientation. Do human beings see themselves as living in subjugation to nature (where nature is perceived to be a powerful force whose decisions over and against humanity can only be accepted), in harmony with nature (with human beings and nature viewed as extensions of one another), or in mastery over nature (where natural forces are to be overcome and put to the use of human beings)?

Time orientation. Do people tend to live in the past (highly valuing the ancestors and traditions), in the present (with little thought for either yesterday or tomorrow), or in the future (with emphasis upon planning and change)?

Activity orientation. Does the culture value "being" (activity that is a spontaneous expression of what is perceived to be the "givens" of the human personality), "being-in-becoming" (activity oriented toward personality development), or "doing" (activity that results in measurable accomplishments)?

Relational orientation. Do the people of a culture value and relate "individually" (with individual goals having primacy over group goals), "collaterally" (with primary emphasis on the welfare of the laterally extended group), or "lineally" (where continuity of the group through time and the ordered positional succession of the group is stressed)?[39]

For the student of congregational life, Redfield's three components of worldview and Kluckhohn and Strodtbeck's five categories of value-orientations provide a helpful starting place for the analysis and categorization of congregational identity. Like any student of any culture the pastor needs to discern the congregation's operative view of God, nature, and humanity. Like any student of any culture, the pastor would be helped by distinguishing the congregation's orientation toward time, activity, and relationships.

However, it should also be acknowledged that congregations not only evidence many of the general characteristics that are found in societal cultures (or subcultures). Congregations, as Christian faith communities, also embody and symbolically communicate a particular *theological* worldview and ethos. And pastors as local theologians are in need of categories that help them discern not only the broader parameters of congregational subcultural life, but also the particular local theologies to which congregations—either consciously or subconsciously—pledge their allegiance.

Informed then, both by Christian theological concerns and by the work of anthropologists such as Redfield, Kluckhohn, and Strodtbeck, we will now consider seven categories, seven "lenses," through which pastors can approach congregational symbols and begin to make assessments—both anthropologically and theologically—regarding congregational worldview and values.

Interpreting Congregational Worldview and Values

1. View of God (Theology, Christology, Pneumatology)

- Is God perceived by this congregation to be primarily transcendent or primarily imminent? (What is the congregation's favorite hymn: "Immortal, Invisible, God Only Wise?" or "What a Friend We Have in Jesus"?)
- Is God most likely to be thought of: as judge and giver of law who exacts high standards for righteous behavior and exhibits wrath toward those who fall short? as merciful and forgiving parent who is quick to understand and forgive foolish ways? or as one in whom both justice and mercy co-exist?
- Is God perceived to regularly intervene directly into human affairs through the working of miracles? Or does God work primarily through natural processes? (How are prayers of intercession phrased in congregational life?)
- Is any one person of the Trinity valued more highly than another? Is any one person of the Trinity consistently devalued in congregational life?
- What metaphors for God (Holy One, Judge, Shepherd, Father, Rock, Mother Eagle), for Christ (Bread of Life, Light of the World, Son of God, Friend of the Poor, Savior, Suffering Servant), and for the Holy Spirit (Wind, Fire, Healer, Empowerer, Giftgiver) are most prevalent in congregational life, and what do they indicate about the congregation's understanding of God?

In the multichurch parish that I served as pastor, three of the four congregations held an annual Christmas pageant. Over time I began to realize that much of what each congregation believed about Jesus was communicated symbolically through its pageant.

The first congregation—an old, historic church—always had an intergenerational gathering of children, youth, and adults playing the various assigned roles in the Christmas story. However, when it came to the role of the baby Jesus, the inviolable tradition was that no real baby or even a baby doll would take the part. Rather, this congregation, reflecting its metaphorical understanding of Jesus as "light of the world," placed a light within the manger—a light that shone forth and reflected the aura of God's own Son come to earth at Christmas. Obviously, the Christology in this church was high. Jesus may have appeared on earth in human form, but to this people he was primarily *God with us.*

In the second congregation, the expectation for the annual Christmas pageant was that a real, live baby would play the role of Jesus. However, it was also expected that the baby would be good: "The little Lord Jesus, no crying he makes." Jesus, then, was a human being, but he was also a superhuman human being (not the kind who had messy diapers, cried when hungry, and shared other human limitations).

In the third congregation, a rural church comprised primarily of dairy farming families, one of the first responses I received when I announced that I (the pastor) was pregnant and that the baby was due in November was, "Hallelujah! We'll have a real baby for the Christmas pageant this year." In this congregation it mattered not whether the baby cried through the entire pageant, wet its diaper, or liberally spit up on Mary. What was most important was that the Word became *flesh* and dwelt among us, and that through one Jesus of Nazareth we could learn how to be more fully human, too.

2. View of Humanity (Theological Anthropology)

- *What is the predominant view of human beings?* (Are people primarily considered to be "sinners without hope save in God's sovereign redemption through Jesus Christ," to be "children of God, created in God's image, loved and recreated through Jesus Christ," or to be "fallible yet perfectible through the inner workings of the Holy Spirit"?)

Tom Long, my friend and colleague in the field of homiletics, tells the story of an elderly Presbyterian minister who used to ask every candidate for ministry that came before his presbytery for examination the same question, "Look out that window and spot a human being you don't know. Now, tell me theologically, what do you see?" Over time the minister said the answers he received fell into one of two categories. Either the candidate responded, "I see a child of God, created in God's own image, loved immeasurably by God, and restored to a right relationship with God through Jesus Christ." Or, the candidate responded, "I see a sinner, worthy of God's judgment and displeasure, and without hope save in God's sovereign mercy." "Neither answer," said the minister, "was a wrong answer, but over time I noticed that the candidates who responded the first way tended to make the kinder pastors." My suspicion is that congregations who respond the former way are also kinder churches.

- *How does this congregation see itself in relation to the rest of society?* (Does it view itself as being primarily powerful or powerless? As being a potential change agent, or as being a victim of circumstances with little power to effect change?)
- *What does this congregation value in human nature: being* (where the worth of an individual is bound up with his/her existence as a child of God), *doing* (where the worth of an individual is closely tied to his/her achievements), or *being-in-becoming* (where primary value is placed upon the individual's personal and spiritual growth)?

3. View of Nature (Theology of Creation)

- *What is the congregation's understanding of creation and the place of human beings within it?* Is the congregation's basic stance toward nature one of:
  a. Harmony with nature (as in many farming communities where people live close to the land and recognize their absolute dependence upon the cycles of seasons, rain, and sunshine for their daily sustenance);
  b. Mastery over nature (as in many urban and suburban contexts in which a major concern is whether nature—that is, rain or sleet, heat or cold—is going to interfere with human plans and activities for the weekend); or
  c. Subjugation to nature (as in areas regularly visited by life-destroying natural disasters, such as hurricanes, tornadoes, earthquakes, or floods)?
- *How would this congregation describe the manner in which human beings ought to live in relation to nature?* (What interpretation of the meaning of human "dominion" in relation to creation is reflected in the signs and symbols of congregational life?)

4. View of Time (Eschatology)

- Is time primarily viewed as a qualitative commodity to be managed, used expediently and not wasted (so that worship or a committee meetings must begin and end according to the clock, and proceed with as much efficiency as possible), as an obstacle to be endured or overcome on the path to a fuller existence (as in "doing time" in the prison), or as a relational entity (so that worship or a meeting begins when the whole community has gathered and proceeds until the community has a corporate sense that it is time to close)?

- Is the congregation primarily oriented to the past (reliving and longing for the "glory days" of long ago); the present (living in such a day-to-day survival mode that it gives little thought either to the past or the future), or the future (with plans and dreams and visions of what it would like to be and do)?

- What is the character of congregational "hope" and how is it related to biblical images of hope (such as "eternal life," "parousia," or "resurrection")?

5. View of the Church (Ecclesiology)

- What metaphors for the church predominate in congregational life? (Is the church primarily conceived as being "institution of salvation," "intimate community of the Spirit," "sacrament of salvation," "herald of good news," or "servant of the servant Lord"[40]?)

- Is the church understood by members of the congregation to be primarily a "hospital for sinners" (where people are welcomed, whatever their life situation, and few restrictions are placed on church membership) or a "holy community of saints" (in which certain ethical standards of lifestyle are required for faithful church membership?)

- How inclusive is the congregation—in its leadership, worship, and programming—of those who are frequently marginalized in the larger society (children, the elderly, women, persons with physical and mental disabilities, gay and lesbian persons, persons of diverse racial and ethnic identities)?

6. View of Christian Mission (Evangelism, Missiology, Social Ethics)

- *If you were going to locate the congregation's own understanding of itself in relation to the larger culture, how would you characterize it?* (Using H. Richard Niebuhr's categories in *Christ and Culture*, would this church's stance toward culture be characterized as "against," "above," "of," "in paradox," or "transforming"[41]?)
- *Would the congregation's mission orientation best be characterized as:*
  a. activist (with strong emphasis on the congregation's own corporate address of social, political, and economic issues),
  b. civic (encouraging church groups to study public issues and encouraging individuals to become involved, while avoiding corporate stands as a church body),
  c. evangelistic (with primary emphasis upon the call of individuals to salvation and eternal life), or
  d. sanctuary (providing a place in which its participants can withdraw from the trials of societal life and find a safe haven)?[42]
- *Would the congregation's own self-image for social ministry best be described as:*
  a. survivor church (reactive to the crises of an overwhelming world);
  b. crusader church (proactive in seeking out issues and championing causes);
  c. pillar church (anchored in its community and taking responsibility for the community's well-being);
  d. pilgrim church (caring for immigrants with ethnic, national, or racial roots), or
  e. servant church (caring for and supporting individuals in need)?[43]

7. Interrelationships among the Above Concerns (Cosmology, Soteriology, Doctrine of Revelation)

- *What overarching view does the congregation have of the cosmos, God's relationship to it, and their place within it?*

Utilizing categories developed by literary critic Northrop Frye, James Hopewell has outlined four worldview orientations he has observed in mainline U.S. congregations.[44] While they are not exhaustive, they are suggestive of the subcultural and theological diversity that can exist among mainline congregations that appear, on the surface, to be very similar.

a. Comic/gnostic. In a cosmic/gnostic worldview, the world at first seems disintegrated and illusory, but through gnosis (inner knowing) the believer comes to discern its unity and purpose. Those who live within the world need to deepen their consciousness of its inner meanings through meditative practices. Peace is to be found by getting in touch and harmony with basic cosmic forces. The gnostic view is marked by phrases or signs such as, "It will all work out," "possibility thinking," holistic healing practices, meditative acts, and artifacts and gestures that encourage a contemplative life. The polar opposite of the gnostic view is the "tragic/canonic" view.

b. Tragic/canonic. In a tragic/canonic worldview, the world is perceived to be unpredictable and inevitably cruel, ultimately ending in death. Human beings are sinful, depraved, and destined for hell unless they repent. The only way for human beings to survive in such a world is to submit to the will and laws of God revealed in the Scriptures. Salvation is to be found through dying to self and to worldly "natural" impulses, and taking up the cross after Christ. Phrases and signs that indicate a canonic worldview are "Bible-believing," "Get right with God," references to moral decay and damnation, and acceptance of illness and catastrophe as a part of God's plan.

c. Romantic/charismatic. Like the gnostic orientation, a romantic/charismatic worldview is basically optimistic. However, the basis for its trust differs. Instead of trusting in an order and unity of the world as God created it, the charismatic trusts in a God who is able to set aside natural processes through miraculous interventions. The journey a Christian takes through life is perilous and dangerous. However, God honors Christians by providing them with a Spirit who miraculously intervenes to conquer evil. The romantic worldview is marked by phrases and signs such as "Expect a miracle," "God told me to. . . ," "I want Jesus to be my Lord and not just my Savior," healings requiring touch and prayer, visions, glossolalia. Its polar opposite is the "ironic/empiric" worldview.

d. Ironic/empiric. The ironic/empiric person believes that all that happens in the world can be explained naturally and scientifically, and that "miracles" don't happen. Truth is to be discerned by relying on the senses, not via revelation. Human beings are basically good, but are trapped in a chaotic, unjust world. The only way to survive is to embrace others in communities of love and support, and to do what one can to make the world a better place for others. The ironic/ empiric view is marked by phrases and signs such as "not holier than thou," "being honest and realistic," "becoming all one can be," "relevance to everyday life," attention to issues of justice, emphasis upon fellowship, acceptance of illness and catastrophes as facts of life.

Interpreting Congregational Ethos

While the questions and categories above can help the local pastor deepen his or her understanding of what a congregation perceives to be "really real" (worldview) and what a congregation values, to describe the overarching "character" or "ethos" of a congregation may require a more imaginative, integrative, and holistic judgment on the part of the pastor. As the proverbial story of the elephant and its five examiners illustrates, unless one steps back from the elephant and an intensive examination of its various parts long enough to peruse and ruminate about the whole, the very nature of the elephant (and the very character of "elephantness") may be lost in the interpretive process.

When pastors discuss congregational ethos, they frequently resort to metaphorical language in order to capture the mood or tone of congregational life. In recent months I have heard pastors describe their various congregations as being "schizophrenic," as "having a good heart," or as "hiding their dirty linen behind a facade of gentle respectability." Recognizing that prose alone is not sufficient for capturing the spirit of congregations, pastors search for descriptions which are more imagistic in nature. Yet while all of these phrases are indicative of congregational character, they are also in need of further expansion within the framework of the congregation's own story in order to become fully intelligible.

Perhaps that is why James Hopewell has argued that it is only within a narrative framework that congregational character can be most adequately described. It is not enough, says Hopewell, to compile a list of personality traits related to congregational character, to summarize the results of a questionnaire about the current congregational "climate." Such approaches provide "no framework for understanding the relation of the traits to each other or to a coherent whole." Rather, descriptions of congregational ethos need to be made narratively, recognizing that "it is primarily in narrative that the character of the congregation emerges as an authentic figure that embodies and historically enacts a variety of traits."[45]

The narratives that Hopewell deems most promising for interpreting congregational ethos are the myths of ancient Greece and Rome. Because myth is a vehicle that people have used throughout history to give expression to their deepest beliefs concerning who they are and who they strive to be, Hopewell believes myth also has special capacity for describing congregational character in the present. Therefore, he urges students of congregational life to search for an appropriate myth within the Greco-Roman tradition which, in an analogous and metaphorical way, can be interpretive of a congregation's subcultural character.

How does the congregational exegete locate the appropriate myth for interpreting his or her congregation? Hopewell encourages attention to four elements that are particularly disclosive of character.

1. *Crisis and integration*: In a loss or dislocation, what is the characteristic response and reintegration that is sought?
2. *Proficiency*: What is the characteristic skill, the chosen manner of doing things, the reliable pattern of behavior?
3. *Mood*: What is the characteristic temperament, the emotional atmosphere?
4. *Hope*: What end is characteristically expected and sought?[46]

An appropriate myth will exhibit these four elements in a manner that is consonant with the congregation's own story.

While acknowledging the dangers of a mythic description of congregational character (the potential of stereotyping, for example) Hopewell also sees positive benefits to be gained. The use of myth can assist a congregation in speaking more concisely (and metaphorically) about its character. The use of myth can help a congregation locate its own story within the larger stories of humanity. And the use of myth can provide the kind of "poetic jolt" that allows people to see their own congregation in fresh terms.[47]

Although I am highly sympathetic with Hopewell's encouragement of a mythic interpretation of congregational character and his assessment of the positive values that can be gained, I find his sole reliance upon Greek and Roman myths to be problematic on several fronts. First, many congregations and pastors have little in-depth knowledge of Greco-Roman myths and are not able to call them readily to memory when looking for congregational analogues. Second, the myths themselves reflect the worldview and values of two very particular Western and ancient cultures, and do not do justice to the plethora of myths that could be used from other cultures and subcultures—ancient and modern. Finally, the narratives that link diverse subcultural Christian congregations, and that give them a common language for speaking about the character of their life and faith, are not the tales of Greek and Roman gods and goddesses, but the stories of the God revealed through the witness of the Old and New Testament Scriptures. It seems a shame to go solely to other religious traditions for stories capable of describing congregational character, when our own tradition is so rich in them.[48]

In recent years, as I have worked with both seminary students and local pastors in the analysis of congregations, I have encouraged them to use Hopewell's mythic approach for an assessment of congregational character, but I have also urged them to make use of any cultural or religious stories or myths (broadly defined) known to them which enable them to summarize the essence of congregational character in a meaningful narrative form. As a result I have heard congregational character described in relation to:

- *fairy tales* (as in the case of the suburban congregation that started out well in life, was lulled into sleep for a number of years, and had only recently been awakened by its "prince charming" pastor);
- *biblical stories* (as in the case of the urban African American congregation, whose history of banishment and betrayal by the congregation from which it splintered was likened unto the story of Hagar and Ishmael);

- *epic novels* (as in the case of the insulated small-town congregation in Georgia whose love/hate relationship with its current pastor was likened unto the stormy relationship between Rhett Butler and Scarlett O'Hara in *Gone With the Wind*);
- *movies* (as in the case of an aging congregation which had recently received rejuvenation akin to that of the elderly characters who frolicked in a swimming pool in the closing scene of the movie *Cocoon*);
- *songs* (as in the case of a small-town congregation in the heart of country music land, whose past shame and current struggle for self-esteem was echoed in the words of the Garth Brooks song, "Learning to Live Again"),
- and *Greek mythology* (as in the case of the struggling blue-collar congregation which, like Sisyphus, never could seem to get the large rock all the way up the hill without a significant setback).

While not always "mythic" in the classic sense of the term, each of these narrative analogues has proved capable of summing up in a fresh way something of the current ethos of congregational life while, at the same time, opening the way for contemplation of the congregation's potential future. Each story has also provided the exegete with a holistic and imaginative way in which to integrate many of the disparate meanings gleaned through thick description of congregational symbols.

Rather than narrowly prescribing the types of myths by which congregational character can be interpreted, much can be said for allowing the pastor's own imagination to roam freely in the quest for a fitting analogue. The goal should not only be to identify a myth that "works" for the preacher, but also (if possible) to discover a storied mirror into which the congregation itself can look and truthfully exclaim, "Yes, this is who we are."

Conclusion

Preaching as "local practical theology" not only requires of its practitioners skill in the exegesis of biblical texts; it also requires facility in the exegesis of congregational contexts. In this chapter we have proposed that preachers become amateur ethnographers, utilizing a symbolic approach to the study of congregational subcultures in order to "thickly describe" their particular identities. In order to assist the pastor in this task we have (*a*) identified some of the signs and symbols of congregational life which hold particular promise for subcultural exegesis, and (*b*) recommended categories and frameworks through which the pastor, as symbolic exegete, can begin to assess and interpret the various dimensions of congregational identity (worldview, values, and ethos). The goal in such exegesis is not only heightened cultural understanding of a general nature, but also greater awareness of previous local theologies that exist in congregational life.

However, the preacher as theologian is concerned with more than discerning and describing the "givens" of congregational life; she or he is also concerned for congregational transformation in light of the worldview, values, and ethos of the Christian gospel. It is then toward the task of theological construction for preaching—the engagement of the horizons of biblical texts and congregational context in a fitting and transformative way—that we now turn our attention.

4
Preaching as Local Theology

Douglas John Hall tells of an airplane trip he took on which a seatmate asked him to describe his work as a theologian. After Hall attempted to answer the query in a responsible way, the passenger earnestly responded, "It must be wonderful to think about everything, all the time!"[1]

At the heart of both the joy and the challenge of Christian preaching is the reality that it requires of the pastor as local theologian both a willingness and an ability to "think about everything, all the time." Christian preaching is an integrative and constructive endeavor, requiring creativity, imagination, and tough, disciplined thinking by those who undertake it on a weekly basis. The pastor who sits in the study, mulling over the upcoming sermon for Sunday, ponders many things at once: the joys and sorrows of individual parishioners, tensions and celebrations in congregational life as a whole, concerns related to the larger church and world, and the pastor's own personal struggles. It is within the crucible of these many contextual concerns that the preacher must think theologically, bringing biblical text and contemporary context together toward proclamation that is "fitting" for a particular place and time.

In this book we have focused upon one significant context that the preacher as local theologian must consider—namely, the congregation and its subcultures with its distinctive worldview, values, and ethos—and have encouraged a process for sermon preparation that takes congregational "contextuality" as seriously as it does biblical "textuality." In chapter 3 we considered ways in which the pastor as "ethnographer" can exegete a local congregation by attending closely to the signs and symbols of its corporate life. Certainly a first step in aiming toward greater contextuality in preaching is for pastors to enhance their own awareness of the subcultural worlds their congregations inhabit, to become more cognizant of the previous local theologies that are extant in congregational life, and (consequently) to become more aware of those junctures at which the preacher's own beliefs, values, and assumptions differ from those of the congregation.

However, enhanced understanding of congregational subculture is only a first step in the contextual process. The local preacher must also ask, "What difference does congregational subculture make—both for the theology of the sermon (the focus of this chapter) and for its art (the focus of chapter 5)? How can the sermon be crafted in such a way that—in its content, language, and form—it is both more "seriously imaginable" and more transformative of local congregations and their assumed worlds?

In this chapter we turn toward the task of theological construction for preaching. Viewing preaching as an act of constructing "local theology," we will explore some ways in which greater consideration of the congregation throughout the sermon preparation process can foster the shaping of a genuinely contextual theology for proclamation. At stake is the method by which pastors approach the hermeneutics of preaching, that process through which the worlds of biblical text and congregational context are brought together in theological proclamation.

While at least one contextual theologian likens the interpretive process to that of following a "map,"[2] I prefer to think of it as engaging in a "dance" of the imagination. The preacher, a key partner in the dance, joins hands with other significant partners—Scripture, congregational context, church doctrine—bending, twisting, and turning with them until the shape and contours of a genuinely local theology begin to emerge. The dance does not always begin in the same place, nor does it always proceed through the same series of steps in a 1-2-3 order. Rather, the preacher as dancer is given freedom to attend to the various partners, and to discern in each new setting in time and place where to begin the dance toward a sermon, and how to proceed. What is important is that all the partners be engaged in each dance, and that their various roles in shaping the dance be defined in a manner which leads toward proclamation that is both faithful to the gospel and fitting for the context.

Partners in the Dance of Contextual Interpretation

The Preacher

The preacher's role in the dance of local theological construction is a dual one. The preacher, on the one hand, is a dance partner, engaging the other partners and being engaged by them in the rigorous discipline and unmitigated joy of dance. On the other hand, the preacher is also charged with the task of imaginative choreography—bringing biblical text, church tradition, and congregational context together into one proclamation of local theology and folk art that is integrative and capable of capturing the imaginations of its hearers. At its best, the Sunday morning sermonic dance inspires others, making them want to put on their own dancing shoes and join in the steps of faith.

In order to participate fully in the dance of interpretation, the preacher, too, must risk being changed. One does not dance very closely with Scripture under the ongoing inspiration of God's Spirit without being addressed—and potentially transformed—by the encounter. In like manner, one does not dance very closely with local congregations—attending to their questions, struggles, insights, and challenges to the preacher's own theology—without also being changed by the encounter. To enter the dance fully requires of the preacher a certain abandonment to its rhythms, a willingness to become so passionately engaged in the dance that its cadences actually reshape and redirect the preacher's own steps.

But engagement in the hermeneutical task also requires of the preacher another kind of risk: the risk of making interpretive leaps with no certainty that the leaper will land on solid ground. Contextual hermeneutics consistently compels the preacher to make decisions—for one thing and against another—with no guarantees that the interpreter is "right." Indeed, interpretive decisions that are "right" (here defined as both faithful and fitting) in one context may prove to be wrong in the next.

When preaching is viewed as local theology, the road to sermon preparation is fraught with risky choices. The choice as to where one will begin sermonic reflection (with biblical text, with a doctrinal concern, or with a current issue in church or world) is a contextual choice. The choice of interpretive methodologies—regarding both text and context—is a contextual choice. The choice of a theological theme for sermonic focus—given the various potential themes that emerge among the dance partners—is a contextual choice. And at every juncture choices for one thing also involve choices against others. The interpretive task regularly requires of the preacher a willingness, amid prayer and faithful inquiry, to make tough decisions and to leap, trusting oneself and one's congregation to a God who is fully capable of using even our missteps to God's glory.

The Bible

"Faith may be an imaginative act," writes Barbara Brown Taylor, "but the Bible reminds us that we are not free to imagine anything we like. . . . By keeping us rooted in our historical tradition, the Bible helps us to know the difference between imagination and delusion; by tethering our own imaginations to that of the whole people of God, the Bible teaches us to imagine the God who was and is and who shall be."[3]

In the dance of interpretation for contextual preaching, Scripture is a leading partner. To say that Scripture takes a "lead" does not imply that the preacher must always begin preparation for contextual preaching with the exegesis of a biblical text, or that Scripture alone determines appropriate themes for proclamation. Rather, it is to suggest that Scripture—because it embodies in its stories and images the normative Christian paradigms of who God is and how God relates to the world—plays a lead role in shaping and transforming the imaginations of Christian communities. The church through the ages has confessed in faith that through the witness of these books and their very human authors, we gain, through the Spirit's workings, a paradigmatic vision of who God is and how God relates to our world.

The task of contextual preaching, then, is to interpret the paradigmatic vision of God, humanity, and the world given in Scripture in a manner that is both faithful to Scripture (in its whole and parts) and also capable of capturing and transforming the imaginations of a particular congregation of hearers. Thus, the question for contextual Christian preaching is not whether one uses Scripture; without Scripture and the One to whom it witnesses preaching has no life.

The question, rather, is how, given particular congregational contexts, the preacher should go about selecting, analyzing, and engaging biblical texts in the dance of interpretation.

The hermeneutical methodology for biblical preaching fostered in many seminaries and practiced by many pastors is one in which the congregation does not become a significant factor in the interpretive process until late in the game. Pastors are taught to begin their sermon preparation by the exegetical study (ordinarily by means of the historical-critical method) of a given text. Next they are to elicit from the text theological themes fruitful for proclamation. Finally, pastors are to reflect upon how those theological affirmations might be applied and communicated in their own congregational contexts.

When preaching is viewed as local theology, the congregation is engaged in the hermeneutical conversation from the outset—much earlier and more deeply than the text-to-theme-to-application approach allows. From the selection of appropriate biblical texts for proclamation, to the methodologies used for interpreting texts, to the discernment of themes for preaching, the congregation plays an active role. The pastor not only engages in "priestly listening" to the biblical text on behalf of the congregation with its own distinctive subculture. The pastor also approaches text selection and interpretation in the mode of "priestly questioning," asking the questions and raising the issues that arise out of congregational life.

In addition, a contextual focus in preaching reminds us that Scripture itself is comprised of a series of local theologies. The four Gospels were contextually shaped for widely divergent faith communities, as were the epistles of Paul and the writings of Jahwist, Elohist, Priestly, and Deuteronomic authors of the Hebrew Scriptures. As Leander Keck reminds us, Scripture itself is "a library of mostly multi-layered literature . . . affected by many cultures and written in three languages for communities of faith in a great variety of situations."[4] While local preachers will not want to lose sight of the canonical "whole" we call the Bible, they will also be reminded that the Bible itself—in its various parts—not only gives license and incentive for contextual preaching; it also provides us with diverse models for constructing and reinterpreting local theologies.

Congregational Subculture

When preaching is viewed as local theology, Scripture is not interpreted in isolation, but in dialogue with the experience and perspectives of a local community of faith. Thus, congregational subculture
becomes an active and highly significant partner in the dance of theological construction. The question is, What role can and should
congregational experience play in the dance?

In his discussion of the various components of a contextual theological methodology, Douglas John Hall outlines and critiques two
current and opposing theological viewpoints regarding the role of
experience in theological construction. In liberal theology, which has
characteristically had a great concern for contextuality and dialogue
with the larger world outside church boundaries, experience has
often been regarded as "the touchstone of theological truth. What
corresponds with human experience is acceptable, what does not
should be discarded as irrelevant."[5]

Despite the many contributions liberal theologies have made to
contextualization, Hall rightly notes that the danger of giving experience such a normative role in theological formation is that there is
nothing left by which experience itself can be judged. "When experience becomes the primary canon of authenticity in theology, the disciple community is robbed of a vantage point from which to reflect
critically upon . . . experience [itself]."[6]

On the other hand, neo-orthodoxy—with its distrust of experience as theological norm and its emphasis on the authoritative role
of God's revelation in Scripture—gave way in time to a theological
methodology that denied experience a significant role in theological
construction. "Everything could be understood from within the circle of faith, it was no longer necessary to go into the marketplace; or,
if one went there, one knew pretty well in advance what one would
find."[7] While neo-orthodoxy made gains in returning the church to
the constancy of its faith as revealed in Scripture, it lost ground in
terms of relevancy. Experience became at best suspect, at worst
unnecessary in theological formulations.

My own quest in the dance of interpretation is for a contextual
"middle way" between these two approaches: an approach that values
(with liberalism) the importance of forging theology in continual
dialogue with the realities of congregational experience, while also
valuing (with neo-orthodoxy) the role of Scripture in providing the

normative paradigms by which experience itself can be evaluated and judged. If preaching is to be both "faithful" and "fitting," then both elements are critical for its theological formulation.

In *Homiletic* David Buttrick makes this bold assertion: "Biblical preaching that will not name God out of narrative and into the world is simply *un*biblical."[8] Engagement with the congregation and its subculture throughout the sermon preparation process not only helps to insure that the preacher will "name God in the world." It also encourages the preacher to name God in the world *the congregation actually imagines.*

Doctrinal Traditions

One of the professors who first introduced me to the wonderful world of homiletics used to bemoan the fact that pastors often rely too heavily on their own limited theological formulations in the sermon preparation process, and do not take time to place their own interpretations of biblical texts into dialogue with broader church traditions of past and present. He reminded seminarians of the great company of faithful witnesses who have gone before us, of the deep roots from which we have sprung as Christians, and encouraged us to build our own pastoral libraries so that when we sat in our studies pondering the Sunday sermon, we were not alone—but were at table with individuals and church bodies who had wrestled with similar issues in other times and places. He also reminded us of the importance of our own particular denominational roots for preaching, and encouraged us to be faithful in sermon preparation to ordination vows in which we (as Presbyterians) pledged to be "instructed and led by" the "essential tenets" of our denominational confessions in our pastoral leadership of the people of God.[9]

Preaching as local theology certainly values such engagement with church tradition. Proclamation is a communal act, which arises not only out of the local congregation but also out of the midst of denominations and a larger Christian community that extends throughout time, space, and eternity. Wise pastors do not craft local theology in isolation, but do so in conversation with the wisdom of the church through the ages. Such engagement holds local theology accountable to a larger church and world, deepens its engagement with and understanding of local issues, and reminds the preacher of some of the boundaries and parameters that have been established for the theological dance floor by the church universal and by particular denominations.

Yet preaching as local theology also encourages a more ecumenical and multicultural consideration of church doctrine than has sometimes been the case in homiletical practice. One of the dangers that arises when pastors consult only doctrines of their own denominational traditions or theologians with whom they already agree is that preaching may simply reinforce local worldviews and values, rather than also challenging and stretching them. Catherine and Justo Gonzalez call this the "Lone Ranger" approach to preaching,[10] in which the preacher largely ignores the "Tontos"—the "different ones"—who are also fellow travelers on the pilgrimage of faith and can bring very different perspectives to bear upon the interpretive process.

By contrast, a genuinely contextual hermeneutic recognizes with Walter Brueggemann that every act of biblical interpretation is both an act of faith and an act of vested interest—a "vested interest that we ourselves are not always able to discern."[11] Therefore the pastor is encouraged to seek out and to engage a diversity (historically, geographically, ecclesially, racially, genderwise, and socioculturally) of theological dance partners in the interpretive process—so that the preacher's and the congregation's own "vested interests" might be illumined, examined, and challenged.

Further, a contextual approach to church traditions reminds us that doctrinal formulations are themselves "local theologies"—forged in response to specific contexts, questions, and issues that have emerged in the life of local communities of faith. Rather than turning previous local theologies into "ideologies"—dogmatically normative in their particular applications for every time and place—a contextual approach reminds us that doctrinal formulations need to be continually interpreted and reinterpreted in a manner that is respectful both of the original context out of which they arose, and of the new context in which they are being considered.[12]

Finally, a contextual hermeneutic also recognizes that doctrinal traditions not only inform local proclamation; local theologies (including those articulated in sermons) also help to re-form and redefine the boundaries of doctrinal traditions. The issues, themes, questions, and concerns raised by local congregations have frequently caused larger church bodies to rethink and reformulate their own doctrinal positions. (In my own denomination, for example, the decision of several local congregations to provide "sanctuary" for illegal and endangered immigrants eventually pushed the entire denomination to rethink its theological and ethical understanding of "sanctuary.") Indeed, sometimes preaching must intentionally cross traditional doctrinal boundary lines in faithfulness to a gospel that is always larger than any particular theological formulation of it, and in response to a context which demands it. While we never do so lightly or cavalierly, there are times, occasions, and contexts which press us to stretch, question, or challenge the established boundaries of the theological dance floor.

From Con/Text to Sermon: Sermon Preparation Revisited

Sermon preparation is often referred to as a "text-to-sermon" process. However, when preaching is viewed as local theology, the process is more accurately described as moving from "con/text" (a term that can mean either "context," or "with the text," or both) to sermon. The pastor undertakes the dance of interpretation with an ongoing and ever-deepening awareness of congregational context, which informs each phase of the interpretive process—from the selection of biblical text(s) for preaching, to the discernment of themes for local proclamation. Let us revisit, then, the stages of the sermon preparation process, and see how the type of contextual dance outlined above might influence decisions made at each juncture.

Selection of Biblical Text(s) for Preaching

Earlier in this century, the most significant debate regarding text selection for much Protestant preaching in the United States was whether one would adopt a "textual" (sometimes called "expository") or a "topical" approach to sermon preparation. That is, would the preacher begin the sermon preparation process with a biblical text and then explicate its meaning for the contemporary world? Or would the preacher begin the sermon preparation process with a theme or issue arising out of contemporary life, and then address it—biblically and theologically—from the pulpit?

Both practices evidenced strengths and weaknesses. While "textual" preaching helped to ground local preaching in the church's normative witness of faith as revealed in Scripture, it was sometimes found lacking in terms of its "contextuality." As Heinz Zahrnt astutely observed in the wake of neo-orthodoxy and its renewed emphasis upon biblical preaching, "On the one hand, without [Barth's theology] present-day preaching would not be so pure, so biblical, and so concerned with central issues, but on the other hand, it would also not be so alarmingly correct, boringly precise, and remote from the world."[13]

"Topical" preaching, on the other hand, made gains in relevancy, but sometimes lost ground biblically and theologically. In the hands of its best practitioners—those capable of bringing the issue at hand into depth conversation with appropriate biblical texts and doctrinal understandings—topical preaching worked well. But in lesser hands, topical preaching feel prey to biblical eisegesis, proof-texting, and proclamation that was limited in scope to the congregation's or preacher's agendas.

What both biblical and topical modes of text selection had in common, however, was that ordinarily it was the local pastor (and the local pastor alone) who determined texts suitable for proclamation on Sunday morning. Consequently, local congregational and pastoral concerns had the potential to play a significant role—whether implicitly in "textual" preaching or explicitly in "topical" preaching—in the text selection process.

The advent of the *Common Lectionary*[14] in 1983, however, inaugurated what has become a highly significant shift regarding text selection by Protestant pastors. Rather than leaving it to the local pastor to determine appropriate texts for preaching, the *Common Lectionary* proposed a series of texts (Old Testament, Gospel, and Epistle)[15] to be used ecumenically by a number of denominations as the basis for proclamation each Sunday of the year.

Today, countless preachers of many denominations have embraced the *Common Lectionary* and use it as a guide for their own text selection in preaching. And they are the first to testify that lectionary preaching has afforded them and their congregations many valuable benefits. Lectionary preaching has pushed pastors to expand their own biblical and theological horizons, and has protected congregations from being fed solely by the whims of the pastor's own preaching preferences (whether textual or topical). Lectionary preaching has relieved preachers of the difficult task of having to decide from "scratch," on a Sunday-by-Sunday basis, which texts to preach. Lectionary preaching has fostered greater congregational appreciation for the cycles of the liturgical year, and has fostered greater ecumenical cooperation and dialogue regarding preaching and worship.

However, despite all the many benefits the lectionary has afforded (and I am one of its many fans), I find somewhat haunting the warning of a pastor friend who, as a Euro-American upper-class female, went to be pastor of a predominantly poor, African American, urban congregation. After serving in her cross-cultural context for several years, and after actually changing her entire style of preaching to accommodate her new congregation, this pastor commented, "I am convinced that a lot of pastors use the lectionary as a cop-out to avoid preaching on issues that need to be addressed in congregational life. They hide behind the lectionary in order to avoid preaching on some of the tough issues facing local congregations, the nation, and the world."

Her concern is echoed in an informal study undertaken by a Midwest graduate student regarding pulpit responses to the Gulf War of 1991.[16] The student picked three sample cities, and phoned their two dozen largest Protestant parishes to see how they addressed the issue from their pulpits that solemn January Sunday after war was decided. He discovered that almost none of the pastors in these churches mentioned the war in their sermons that morning. When asked for an explanation, the usual response given was, "We follow the lectionary."

When preaching is viewed as local theology, we are reminded that one of the values that may have been lost or devalued in the move from a preacher-designed lectionary to an ecumenically designed lectionary is a serious consideration of the local congregation itself in the process of text selection. Lectionary preaching, as valuable as it is, also needs to be tempered by congregational concerns in the text selection process. Indeed, slavish adherence to any preset preaching program—lectionary or otherwise—militates against genuine contextuality. The preacher who "hides behind" a text (lectionary or other) in order to avoid engagement with a crucial congregational concern, is no more virtuous than the preacher who hides behind pet "topics" in order to avoid confrontation with troublesome biblical texts.

What, then, will a contextual hermeneutic look like in the text selection process? First of all, a contextual approach encourages the preacher to make the congregation itself a significant and conscious consideration in the text selection process—whatever method of selection is ordinarily employed. Even lectionary preachers make choices among the various texts proposed for the day, and those choices should also be informed by engagement with the congregation. What are its burning concerns and issues? What are its current struggles and frustrations? Where is its life faithful to the gospel and worthy of affirmation? Where is its theology lacking, and in need of expansion or correction?

Second, a contextual hermeneutic encourages flexibility regarding the appropriate "starting point" in the sermon preparation process. Indeed, in a contextual approach the entire starting point issue—characterized by the "textual" (always start with a biblical text) versus "topical" (always start with an issue arising out of the context) argument—seems more like a chicken-and-egg debate than one of genuine substance. Ordinarily (given Scripture's lead role in the dance of proclamation), the sermon preparation process may well begin with consideration of one of the assigned lectionary passages for the day, in which the local pastor seeks to discern where the text(s) might correct, confirm, or expand congregational imagination. Other weeks the contextual pastor will be called upon to analyze and reflect theologically upon some issue or concern in church or world, and then search for a text or overarching biblical paradigm to address it. Many weeks it will be difficult to tell which came first in text selection—a congregational concern (which informs the pastor's choice among texts for proclamation), or a commitment to proclamation of the whole canon (equally born out of congregational concern for a holistic theology), or both. What remains constant is the goal: the transformation of congregational imagination through proclamation that is rooted in the paradigmatic world revealed in Scripture.

Third, when preaching is viewed as local theology the best laid plans of pastors and other worship planners and leaders can (and must) be interrupted on occasion so that the pulpit can proclaim a relevant and "fitting" word. On April 19, 1995, disaster struck our nation when the Alfred P. Murrah Federal Building in Oklahoma City was bombed. The entire nation watched as burned and bleeding bodies of children and adults were carried from the wreckage. On the

Sunday following the bombing—a day of national mourning for the tragedy, as well as the Second Sunday of Easter—I was struck anew by the power of contextual preaching as I listened to a local pastor set aside the sermon he'd planned to preach, and preach instead on the tragedy.[17]

He began his sermon that Sunday with the question, "Where do we find hope in the face of evil such as this?" (a question much on the congregation's corporate heart), moved to a consideration of "doubting Thomas" and of his difficulty in believing in a God of resurrection in the face of crucifixion, and culminated the sermon with the affirmation that the presence and promise of the risen Christ can be known to us—as it was to Thomas—in the midst of the gathered community on the Lord's Day. As a sign and symbol of that presence, the pastor pointed to the baptism of two children we had celebrated that morning as a congregation, and called us to find there hope in Christ's life-giving presence.

It was a sermon deeply appreciated by the local congregation—in large part because it began where we, the people were (rather than being controlled by any pre-set agenda), but also because it refused to leave us there. We entered the sanctuary that day with an image of a fireman carrying the body of a dying baby from the wreckage of evil seared upon our imaginations (a picture that was widely reprinted in the wake of the disaster). But we left the sanctuary with another image to place beside it: the image of resurrection presence and power made visible to us in the baptism of two of the congregation's own infants.

Preaching as local theology sets aside its own agenda on occasion to boldly address the critical issues of our day. It recognizes those moments in congregational life when it is far better to address a question people are actually asking than to ask one that may or may not have any relevance to their lives in the present moment.

Finally, when preaching is viewed as local theology, the pastor may want to consider ways in which the congregation itself can literally take part in the selection of texts or topics for proclamation. One summer during my pastorate in those four small churches I decided to depart from the lectionary, and to offer my local congregations the opportunity to suggest topics or texts of their choice for my preaching. The sermon requests I received ran the gamut from a sermon on the phrase "he descended into Hell" in the Apostles' Creed, to a sermon on the parable of the laborers in the vineyard (requested by a farmer), to a sermon on Christian ethics in the workplace (suggested by a business person). I am not sure how effective I was in addressing the texts and issues of their choice, but this I do know—I certainly preached that summer on some topics and texts I probably wouldn't have selected for many years (if left to my own devices), and the interest level—especially on the part of those individuals who made requests—was high.

Preacher's Initial Encounter with the Biblical Text

From my work with local pastors and seminarians, I am convinced that one of the practices that gets most shortchanged in the sermon preparation process—and one of the junctures that holds most promise for strengthening contextuality in preaching—is the initial encounter between the preacher and the biblical text. In *Preaching*, Fred Craddock urges pastors to begin their interpretation of biblical texts with a first, naive reading of the text.[18] Before turning to commentaries, lexica, or other aids, the preacher is to spend time with the text as it stands—allowing initial questions, impressions, intuitions, and feelings about the text to emerge and be recorded.

For Craddock, this naive reading serves two important purposes. First, the preacher begins, through this process, to form guesses and hunches about the text's meaning, and thus to "own" the message that will later be preached. If preachers don't take time at the outset to form their own ideas about a text and its possible meanings, they can simply become sponges in the interpretive process, soaking up what everyone else has said about a text without contributing anything of significance to the dialogue.

The second reason Craddock gives for lingering awhile over the initial, naive reading of the biblical text—and one that is particularly relevant for a contextual approach—is that it is in this first reading that the preacher most closely approximates the congregation's own naive hearing of the text when it is read aloud in worship. "Very likely," writes Craddock, "the questions to be pursued [in the sermon] will be those raised by the text itself in this first reading. It is also likely that these early notes [taken during the naive reading] will provide more than half one's introductions to sermons."[19]

Preaching as local theology recognizes with Craddock the vital significance of that first naive encounter between preacher and biblical text. But it also encourages the preacher to approach the initial encounter with biblical text in the dance of interpretation with one hand firmly grasping the congregation's own. If the preacher begins at this early and formative stage of the interpretive process to listen to and question the text—not only on the pastor's own behalf, but also on behalf of the congregation with its own particular worldview and values and ethos—then it is likely that the resulting sermon will also be more engaging, interesting, and "fitting" for that local congregation.

Elizabeth Achtemeier offers four questions that can be helpful guides for the preacher in bringing the worlds of congregation and biblical text together in proclamation. While Achtemeier recommends that the preacher ask these questions after undertaking exegesis of the biblical text, it is critical in a contextual approach to begin asking them much earlier—during the initial naive encounter with the text—so as to forge from the outset a theology that is both faithful and fitting. The questions are:

1. What would my people doubt to be true in this text?
2. What do my people need to know or to be reminded of from this text?
3. With what inner feelings, longings, thoughts, and desires of my people does this text connect?
4. If this text is true, what kind of world do we live in? Or what if this text were not true, what would be the consequences?[20]

Certainly the hunches preachers form during their initial encounters with texts need to be tested through the rigors of serious and scholarly exegesis, and also need to be placed into conversation with the insights of other scholars and theologians. However, if pastors do not begin at the outset of sermon preparation the kind of reflection that brings biblical world and congregational world together, if they do not pause to both listen to and question the biblical text on behalf of a very particular subcultural gathering of people, then it is likely that the theology they construct will also be less than fully contextual.

Methods for Biblical Interpretation

In terms of formal exegetical procedures, a concern for contextuality in preaching presses pastors to explore and make use of newer methods in biblical interpretation that can complement and correct a sole reliance on the historical-critical method. For example, recent sociological approaches to the study of biblical texts can help the preacher see more clearly how texts are themselves examples of diverse "local theologies" and can help prevent local theologians from making too quick or superficial an identification between the community to whom the biblical text was addressed, and the congregation whom the pastor must address.

All too often in preaching the worlds of text and of congregation are prematurely collapsed through statements such as, "We are all just like the Corinthians" or "We are all just like the Pharisees." A more thorough understanding of the sociocultural worlds out of which a biblical text arose can assist the local theologian in differentiating between biblical and congregational worlds (with their attendant idioms, worldviews, and values). Theologies for preaching can also become deeper and more fitting when the preacher asks, "What meaning(s) might this same text have in a very different context?"

New Testament scholar Peter Lampe once gave a lecture at a seminary where we were both on the faculty, in which he examined some of the sociocultural conditions that contributed to the Corinthian church's problematic observance of the Lord's Supper (1 Cor. 11:17-35).[21] His address especially focused upon the way in which Lord's Supper observance in Corinth had been patterned after Greco-Roman dinner parties—parties at which it was common (*a*) for everyone to bring a potluck picnic basket to contribute to the meal, and (*b*) for the meal to take place in two distinct parts (with some guests arriving early to eat both portions, while others arrived only in time for the second). The problem in Corinth, said Lampe, was not intentional rudeness. The problem was that by patterning their eucharistic meals according to their dinner parties, wealthier members of the Corinthian church were able to arrive early and eat the best portions of the dinner, while poorer members—who arrived later and, in some instances, had neither time nor money to prepare sufficient food baskets—went hungry.

One of the seminarians who attended the lecture decided she wanted to preach on this text in her field education congregation.

But she was also aware that her context for proclamation was very different: a relatively homogenous (classwise) congregation in which there was no potluck dinner associated with eucharistic celebration. After engaging awhile in the dance of interpretation, she decided that there was, however, a connecting point between the Corinthian context and her own, and that it was to be found in a similar power dynamic: that is, in both congregations—whether intentionally or not—weaker members of the community were being excluded by more powerful members from full participation in table fellowship. However, in her context the issue was not one of class but of age. Because all elementary-aged children were encouraged to leave worship early in the Sunday morning liturgy to attend a "children's church" class (in part, so that their presence would not disrupt the very formal worship of adults), they were never present when the eucharist was observed. The adults, therefore, were able to feast and drink fully at the Lord's table, while the children—even though their baptism in this denomination afforded them the right to be at table—went away hungry.

The sermon she prepared did encourage the congregation to reconsider its practice. However, rather than indicting her flock with the "we are just like the Corinthians" line (and perhaps raising defenses to a level at which an open hearing would have been precluded), her sermon also included a very sophisticated differentiation between the two contexts. An enhanced understanding of the sociological factors at work in Corinth deepened her understanding of the text, of her own context, and of the text's address to both.

In like manner, literary and symbolic approaches to biblical interpretation—through the attention they give to the poetic and narrative qualities of texts as they now stand—provide deeper insight into the ways in which Scripture's own symbols, images, plots, and characterizations can work (and have worked) to reshape congregational imaginations. Rather than rushing by the words and images on the surface of the text in the quest to discover its deeper cognitive meaning, contextual interpreters will do well to pause and ponder the shape and texture of the text itself—asking where there are consonances and dissonances between the world conveyed in the story and images of the text and the world as lived and experienced by the local congregation, and questioning how the text's own language might trigger and transform congregational imagination.

One of the biggest shifts in my own preaching in recent years has been a move toward greater appreciation of the powerful symbols biblical texts themselves offer the preacher. Where once I rushed by the language of the text in quest of its deeper meaning, now I find myself looking first to the images, phrases, and symbols that the text itself might offer for congregational transformation. Frequently it is those images or symbols that become the organizing centers around which my sermon is crafted.

For example, several years ago when I was invited to preach for a ministers' gathering on a January weekday, I turned first to the daily lectionary passages to see what they might offer. As I went to the texts with my particular congregation in mind, what immediately caught my attention—even in an initial surface reading—were the contrasting images for ministry that emerged from them. In Isaiah 52:7 I read that the feet of those who proclaim good news are "beautiful." Yet in Galatians I read that a frustrated Paul (obviously going through a "January" of his own in his ministry to the Galatians) was "in the pain of childbirth until Christ is formed in you" (Gal. 4:19). The resulting sermon—entitled "Beautiful Feet and Labor Pains"—became an exploration of these two contrasting images for ministry, and a recognition that if we pastors preach the whole gospel of Christ there will be days when people think our feet are beautiful, and days when we, like Paul, will know the labor pains of a blocked birth.

Or, when confronted during Holy Week with preparation of a Good Friday sermon for a congregation which had undergone much pain and loss in the prior year—including the loss of a beloved pastor—I was drawn in John 21 (also a lectionary passage for the day) toward the encounter between Jesus on the cross, his mother Mary, and John the disciple. "What is going on here?" I found myself asking even in an initial reading of the text. "Is there more at stake than simply a son lovingly caring for his mother's welfare as he dies?" My exegesis led me to believe that there was—that in John's Gospel what we have happening at the foot of the cross is a symbolic foreshadowing of the new community to come, in which family ties through Christ extend far beyond those of kinship. Ironically then, here at the cross a new family is being born—even as the beloved son dies. The resultant sermon (entitled "The Death of a Son and the Birth of a Family") became an invitation to wail and lament with Mary on Good Friday all the senseless deaths and losses of our lives (including the congregation's own corporate losses), while also realizing that even in our deepest grief, Christ comes to us in compassion—offering hope and comfort through the new community made possible through his death.

Preaching as local theology not only values sociological and literary exegetical approaches; it also values the "reader responses" diverse local persons and communities have contributed to textual understanding. In his inaugural address at Union Theological Seminary in Virginia, Old Testament scholar W. Sibley Towner made a case for teaching seminarians to engage in what he labeled "holistic exegesis" of biblical texts.[22] Noting the shortcomings of the historical-critical method for theological reflection,[23] Towner argued that seminarians should be taught an exegetical method that integrates concern for what the text "meant" (using historical criticism) with a concern for what the text "means" (with emphasis on reader response). The exegetical process should oscillate "from the text outside to the text inside and back again, from the author's intention to reader's response."[24]

Consequently, Towner pleaded that a place be made in the process of exposition "*for a chronicle of the believing response to the text*"[25]— that is, for a consideration of what the text has meant and continues to mean in the lives of ordinary Christians.

> One cannot know what a text can mean and perhaps does mean until one has listened to righteous interpreters tell about its abiding truth claims and how they applied them in their several generations. We're not simply talking about commentators, either. These interpreters include oral traditioners, homilists, artists, sculptors, and folk singers.[26]

Preaching as "local theology" values, with Towner, the ways in which local persons and faith communities have interpreted Scripture through the ages in response to their own contexts. The Bible does not belong to scholars alone; it belongs to the whole people of God. And the dance of interpretation can be greatly enriched if, in the interpretive process, the pastor joins hands not only with scholars and theologians, but also with poets and artists, with hymn writers and insightful lay people, in the quest for deeper understanding.

Many local pastors have found value in leading weekly Bible studies on upcoming texts for proclamation, and incorporating some of the questions, insights, and observations that actually arise out of local textual study into their Sunday sermons. I am told that Browne Barr, pastor for many years of the First Congregational Church in Berkeley, California, not only met regularly with such a group; he also structured the group so that its membership turned over each year—thus insuring that the same voices were not always heard in the interpretive process. Similar practices offer the preacher an authentic way in which to heighten and highlight the congregation's own role in the shaping of local theologies for proclamation.

But if indeed (as Brueggemann asserts) all biblical interpretation takes place in both faith and vested interest, and if it is a worthy goal that preaching be not only "local" in address, but also "global" in concern and vision, then contextual preachers also need to provide in the interpretive process for ways in which their own vested interests, and those of their congregations, can be checked and challenged within a broader world community. Certainly one way to do so is for the pastor to attend very carefully to the resources with which she or he builds an interpretive library.

Until recently, biblical commentaries were predominantly written by white Western males, and the pastor's exposure to different contextual voices was limited. However, with the increasing emergence of commentaries and theologies written from diverse perspectives— African American, feminist, two-thirds world—it is now very possible for local pastors to build their libraries so that other voices and perspectives can challenge and broaden their own. In the dance of the imagination for local preaching, the dance will only be as lively, as stretching, and as challenging as the partners the preacher is willing to engage in the process. If the room for sermon preparation is peopled with those who share the worldview of the preacher or the congregation, possibilities for expansion of understanding can be limited. But if the room is also populated with those who interpret life and biblical texts in radically different and challenging ways, then the dance can become very interesting indeed—possibly even transformative!

Discerning Themes/Strategies for Local Proclamation

It should be obvious by now that when preaching is viewed as "local theology" its themes arise neither from biblical text alone or from congregational context alone, but from a dance that engages both. Local themes for proclamation grow out of the particular encounter that occurs when a thick description of congregation subculture and an in-depth exegesis of a biblical text meet. This encounter is mediated through the pastor's own imagination, but is also guided, corrected, and informed by encounters with other faithful interpreters of past and present.

While at times themes for proclamation may emerge out of tensions within congregational life itself, or out of tensions within or among biblical texts, a contextual approach encourages the local pastor to look additionally in another direction to find fitting themes for local proclamation—namely, toward *both the consonances and the dissonances that are created when the idiom, worldview, and ethos of the biblical text and the idiom, worldview, and ethos of the congregation meet.*

In order to assist the local pastor in discerning themes for proclamation, I would propose five different strategies for consideration when bringing the worlds of biblical text and congregational context together in shaping local theology. While not exhaustive, these strategies are suggestive of transformative ways in which text and context can meet in proclamation. The choice as to which strategy (or strategies—for often good sermons employ more than one) are most appropriate in any given situation will, of course, be a contextual one.

1. Preaching can affirm and confirm the right imaginings of the congregational heart.

Human beings thrive on affirmation, and the human communities we call congregations are no exception. Congregations (like all of us) love to be told what it is they are doing right—where their own beliefs and values reflect those of the gospel, where their own practices and mission involvements are patterned after the call of Christ, and how their own life together reflects human community in the Spirit.

Yet all too frequently Christian preaching is stingy with such affirmation. As a whole, we preachers tend to be better at telling people where they fall short and are deficient than we are at affirming the ways in which Christ is already manifest in the midst of their corporate life. We are better at naming Christ's presence "out there" than we are at identifying signs and symbols of Christ's presence "here and now"—within the corporate life and activity of the local congregation itself.

One of the great strengths of James Hopewell's approach to congregations is that he encourages pastors and lay people to look for Christ's presence and ongoing activity not only outside the congregation, but also within it. "I gain the impression from some denominational meetings and seminary lectures," writes Hopewell, "that the real church can be located just outside the network of concrete parishes and might well function better without them."

> But the thick gathering that constitutes congregational life is more substantial than is usually acknowledged. . . . Its specific disappointments and predictable sins are real, but they are also the lot of humanity caught everywhere in a story of accomplishment and failure, of devotion and disobedience. . . . The thick gathering of the congregation is much more than a hypocritical assembly; it is for Christians the immediate outworking of human community redeemed by Christ."[27]

Preaching as local theology recognizes the local congregation as "the immediate outworking of human community redeemed by Christ" and looks for Christ's incarnate presence in its midst. When biblical text and congregational context meet, we need to not only ask where congregational imagination falls short in relation to the biblical witness. We also need to ask how, in light of the text, the sermon might affirm and confirm the right imaginings of the congregational heart.

Several years ago the pastor of a small town congregation in eastern North Carolina shared with me a sermon he preached in his local congregation entitled "Makers of Stone Soup."[28] The sermon began with a retelling of the children's story "Stone Soup." In that tale, three tired and hungry soldiers on their way home from battle approach a village and ask its inhabitants for some food. But the villagers, wary of strangers and not anxious to share with them, hide their food instead. Undaunted, the soldiers announce that they will make their specialty, stone soup. They take a large pot, fill it with water, place it over an open fire, and add the "magic ingredient"—three smooth stones—to the rapidly boiling pot. All afternoon the soldiers stir the pot, stopping at various intervals to taste their soup and also to comment on needed improvements, "'Tis good, but a little salt and pepper would certainly help." "Even better if we had a few carrots." "Seems we always include cabbage. No point mentioning cabbage though." After each suggestion for improvement, one of the townspeople contributes the needed ingredient until, at the end of the day, the entire town turns out to feast on what they all declare is the best soup they've ever eaten.

After recounting the "Stone Soup" story, the sermon then moved into affirmation of this congregation's own ability to make stone soup, citing specific stories from their corporate past:

- The story about the Christmas when fifteen inches of snow unexpectedly fell and how, when all other churches in town had closed down, this one stayed open—sending out trucks and other vehicles to bring over one hundred people in to celebrate "stone soup" communion (which had been prepared for forty).
- The story of Luther, a lay leader within the congregation, who stood during a congregational meeting in which the church was struggling to see how it could finance needed renovations and said, "Just begin to build, and the money will come in!"— and how it did, just like the vegetables for stone soup.
- And the story of a former minister, who "almost sinned" by stalking out of a session meeting in anger over a disagreement—until, that is, one of the elders stopped him at the door and said, "You can't go without a prayer. Come back with us." Because, as the elder knew, you can't make stone soup unless everyone participates.

Finally, the sermon moved to the biblical story itself from Matthew 15:21-28, telling how a Canaanite woman who, though initially "as invisible . . . as a transient on the street before 11:00 worship," begged Jesus to cast out her daughter's demon and who, in so doing, pressed the disciples and Jesus to make the soup pot big enough to provide even for Gentiles and the severely possessed. It concluded with encouragement to the congregation to follow Jesus' example and to keep on expanding their own soup pot to include those beyond the realm of "family" and "our own."

The sermon, this pastor reported, was well received by his congregation. So well, in fact, that when the congregation celebrated its

Homecoming Sunday the next fall, they called it "Stone Soup Sunday"—and even had coffee mugs designed to mark the occasion!

Preaching as local theology finds ways to lift up and celebrate past and present faithfulness in congregational life. It names God not only in the world beyond the congregation, but also in the ordinary, everyday world the congregation inhabits—pointing to those small but significant signs and symbols of "right imagining" in the congregation's own corporate life. Such preaching not only builds up the people of God; it also encourages them toward greater faithfulness. Indeed, often the most effective prophets are those who are first able to perceive, to name, and to appreciate the *right* imaginings of the congregational heart.

2. Preaching can stretch the limits of the congregational imagination.

One of the functions of Christian preaching through the ages has been to expand limited understandings of God, church, and world in light of the normative paradigms of Scripture. Often the problem with congregational imagination is not so much with falsehood as it is with boundaries that have been drawn too narrowly around God, church, grace, forgiveness, or law. When text-world and congregational-world meet, transformation sometimes beckons the preacher toward imaginative world expansion.

A congregational Christology that is very high, for example, is not so much in need of correction (from being false) as it is of balance and expansion in light of Jesus' humanity. In like manner, while many congregations would agree that prejudice and racial hatred are antithetical to the Christian faith, most are also in need of enlarged vision and heightened sensitivity regarding the ways in which they still participate and contribute to the very actions and attitudes they abhor.

Several years ago a seminarian, who was serving as minister to youth in a rapidly growing and progressive suburban congregation, sought to stretch her congregation's ecclesiology through a sermon entitled "Family Is Whom You Know."[29] The congregation, which had been founded during the 1960s on the "house church" model (with small groups meeting in the homes of members for worship and a meal), prided itself on being "family" to one another. However, in the '80s and '90s the church had undergone considerable growth in membership and was no longer able to function in the same intimate way it had in the past. Youth and adults alike were complaining that they didn't know people in the church any more, and that a mark of their distinctiveness—being family to one another—was being eroded.

The seminarian began her sermon with a definition of "family" that was comfortable for this congregation, a definition that included blood relatives or close friends—people with whom we have a literal face-to-face relationship. She traced some of the church's history in fostering such relationships, and affirmed the ways in which this body of God's people had cared for one another in the past. She openly named the current tensions in congregational life, asking whether indeed "family" was being sacrificed to growth.

But her sermon also pressed toward a new and enlarged theological understanding of "family," family defined not simply as *those whom we know*, but defined (through the Ephesians text) as *those who know and are known by God*. She illustrated how we can be "kin" to people we don't personally know by recounting an experience at a family wedding where, when the extended families of the bride and the groom all stood together to bless the couple, they were knit together as one by their mutual love and care for the couple. And she assured this congregation that indeed, they too were already family through their common devotion to Jesus Christ. Finally, she moved into a discussion of how this congregation could continue to nurture, strengthen, and expand their familial ties—including their embrace of newcomers in their midst.

Preaching as local theology not only blesses the "right imaginings" of the congregational heart. It also expands and stretches the horizons of congregational imagination in light of the gospel vision. In so doing, it offers both comfort and challenge to its hearers.

In his book *U. S. Lifestyles and Mainline Churches*, Tex Sample recounts a similar experience of contextual world-stretching—though in a very different context and around a different theological issue. The pastor of a congregation previously unknown to Sample invited him to be the guest preacher one Sunday and to address the issue of peacemaking. By telephone the pastor had encouraged Sample to say what was on his heart, to "lay it out" for this congregation. It was only after Sample arrived at the parsonage about nine o'clock on Saturday night that the pastor told him the rest of the story, "By the way, Tex, this is really a 'hawk' church. Half the congregation is military, and the other half is a combination of skilled blue collarites and lower middle-class sales and service people. I thought you might want to know that before tomorrow."[30]

Sample tells of struggling that night to decide how to begin the sermon the next day. But he finally decided to begin it with a story of a cross-country airplane trip he took one cloudless day where he experienced, from coast to coast, the grandeur of America. He began the sermon on common ground, with a love both he and the congregation shared for their land and its peace and beauty. But then he expanded the vision—to include other lands, other beauty, and a dream of a world without nuclear weapons, living at peace.

"Surely many people there disagreed with some, maybe most, of what I said," writes Sample, "but they listened, and when the service ended I received what seemed to be genuine warmth from them and expressions of gratitude that did not seem contrived or forced. I do not think now—and did not think then—that this was some ringing evidence of my skill as a preacher or my oratorical power . . . because what I saw happen was that I made contact with *their* approach to meaning, with *their* love of country, and in that context they trusted me enough to let me say things they otherwise would not have tolerated gladly."[31]

Preaching as local theology sometimes adopts a strategy in which the preacher begins within the confines of the right imaginings of the congregational heart (in this case, with a love of beauty and desire for peace), and then stretches the walls of such imagining to embrace other peoples, places, and instances where such "right imagining" has not yet made its way.

3. *Preaching can invert the assumed ordering of the imagined world of the congregation.*

The parables of Jesus are known for their world-inversion: the laborers hired last are paid equal to the first; the hated Samaritan becomes a hero; the prodigal son has a party thrown in his honor, and the person who saves and stores treasure is labeled a fool. Contextual preaching, likewise, will challenge the assumed ordering of the congregation's imaginative world. False pecking orders, constructed for the protection of vested interests, will be unmasked, and the revolutionary reversals of God's reign announced.

Although I don't remember the details, I still remember the text, theme, and structure of the sermon I heard on July 4, 1976. The setting was a historic downtown congregation in the state capital of a large, southern city—a congregation whose membership was comprised both of "first families of the South" (with forbearers among the first American settlers) and of a number of newer immigrants who worked in state and city governments, courts of law, banking, and other power centers. It was, of course, the nation's bicentennial celebration, and I was deeply curious as to what the pastor of this congregation—known for having a prophetic voice in our city—would say on this day.

The sermon was based on the Luke 20 text "Render to Caesar the things that are Caesar's, and to God the things that are God's." The first half included a recounting of all the wonderful things we as Americans had to be grateful for on this day, and a call to us to "render to Caesar" the gratitude, obedience, and support that was due to Caesar—gratitude for the state as a hedge against anarchy, obedience to the laws essential for our well-being and common life together, and support through our taxes, voting, and other involvements in the political arena. Few objected to the first half of the sermon. Indeed, most were nodding in agreement.

But in the middle of that sermon came a powerful turning point when, in expanding the meaning of the biblical text, the pastor (essentially) said, "The image stamped on the coin is the image of Caesar. But the image stamped on you from creation is the image of God. Therefore you dare not give Caesar your ultimate allegiance, for that belongs only to your Creator—God." And, the rest of the sermon proceeded to spell out—in equally particular ways—some of those areas in which the demands of Caesar and the demands of God might well conflict, and in which we as Christians dare not place any sovereign above our God.

It was a powerful sermon—but one that was not universally acclaimed by that local congregation. For like the parables of Jesus, at the heart of that sermon was a declaration of world inversion. "If you assume a worldview in which country and God stand on the same plane for allegiance or are identical, or if you assume a worldview in which loyalty to country supersedes loyalty to God, think again," this sermon proclaimed. "For in the realm of God's reign, the ordering is quite different."

4. *Preaching can challenge and judge the false imaginings of the congregational heart.*

Contextual preaching not only calls upon the preacher to "name God" in congregational life; it also calls upon the preacher to name idolatry and falsehood in congregation and world. And, as Walter Brueggemann reminds us, often the first response to such preaching is not one of rejoicing and glad embrace, but one of anger, denial, and grieving over the loss of an old way of life.[32] Faithful contextual preaching, then, will necessarily include painful preaching, in which the dance is more appropriate to a funeral—or, perhaps to the frenzied tarantella that comes after being bitten by a spider—than to a resurrection gigue.

In a sermon entitled "The Reuben Option," preached during the midst of the struggle against apartheid in his native South African, Allan Boesak models preaching that dares to name and unmask idolatry within the church itself. Boesak's sermon centers upon Reuben, one of Joseph's brothers who offered a "respectable compromise" when the other brothers wanted to kill Joseph, encouraging them instead to sell him into slavery. In the sermon, Reuben becomes a paradigm for all in the church who, in their quest for respectability, adopt a stance of cowardice in confronting tough issues. Boesak's proclamation, though a highly contextual one, also communicates well across cultures.

> This, I think is the agony of the church: we know what we should be doing, but we lack the courage to do it. . . . We stand accused by a history of compromises always made for the sake of survival.
> We have justified slavery, violence, and war; we have sanctified racism and split our churches on the issue of the preservation of white supremacy. We have discriminated against women and kept them servile whilst we hid our fear of them behind claims of "masculinity" and sanctimonious talk about Adam and Eve. We have grown rich and fat and powerful through the exploitation of the poor, which we deplored but never really tried to stop. All in the name of Jesus Christ and his gospel. Now this same gospel speaks to us, and we can no longer escape its demands. It calls us to love and justice and obedience. We would like to fulfill that calling, but we do not want to risk too much. The Reuben option."[33]

Instead of adopting the Reuben option, Boesak calls upon Christians to follow the lead of Kaj Munk, a Danish pastor who was executed by the Nazis for his anti-Hitler stance, and to take on "a holy rage," remembering that "the signs of the Christian church have always been the lion, the lamb, the dove and the fish. But *never* the chameleon."[34]

Preaching as local theology is not afraid to name idolatry and falsehood in the life of the local congregation, the broader community, the nation, or the world. And occasionally, in the name of the Gospel, the pulpit, too, will sound with a holy rage.

5. *Preaching can help congregations imagine worlds they have not yet seen (or even imagined).*

As preachers, we always stand to speak in an in-between place—between the "already" and the "not yet," between Christ's first coming to earth and the promised culmination of all things in Christ, between realized and yet-to-be-realized eschatology. While we glimpse signs and symbols of God's work in our midst, we still see through a glass darkly, and do not yet perceive the clarity and fullness of that which will be.

One of the tasks of contextual preaching, then, is to assist congregations in imagining that which the Scriptures tell us is still to come, in glimpsing the promised future in such a way that present living can be transfigured. Funerals are often a place in which such imagining occurs in congregational life. As the community gathers to hear biblical texts read that speak of "a new heaven and a new earth," a home with "many mansions," and a place where "mourning and crying and pain will be no more," they are also enabled to envision an alternative world, unlike any they have actually seen.

Walter Brueggemann says that "[t]he purpose of the sermon is to provide a world in which the congregation can live."[35] Preaching as local theology not only offers congregations an alternative world in which to live here and now; it also offers them a world *to live into.*

There is probably no better known or loved world-imagining sermon in recent U.S. history than Martin Luther King Jr.'s "I Have a Dream" speech. Preached from the "pulpit" of the Lincoln Memorial in our nation's capital, King's speech was a highly contextual sermon, proclaimed to a national congregation. Its profound power lay not only in its rich cadences and stirring rhetoric, but also in its capacity to create a world this nation as yet could only imagine—but a world for which many hungered and yearned. King gave us a world to live into.

Preaching as local theology also gives local congregations new worlds to live into. If the imagined world is one of exclusion and prejudice, then preaching needs to paint an alternative world in which there is no Jew nor Greek, slave nor free, male or female—but all are one in Christ Jesus. If the imagined world is one of violence and fear, then preaching needs to portray a world in which wolf and lamb lie down together, and children play around serpents without harm. If the imagined world is one of mourning and terror, then preaching needs to portray an alternative world, one in which a voice cries, "Comfort, comfort my people," and in which springs break forth in the desert. If the imagined world is one of powerlessness and oppression, then preaching needs to paint an alternative world—one in which God miraculously parts waters, leads people from slavery to freedom, and pronounces death upon all forces of evil that would hurt or destroy.

In 1979, in the midst of the Cold War, the local pastor of an urban congregation that included many business and community leaders, preached a sermon based on the story of God's covenantal sign to Noah, the rainbow. The questions the sermon addressed were highly contextual ones for the time and place, "Has the cracking of the atom and the invention of nuclear weapons destroyed the magic of the rainbow? Has the possibility of a nuclear holocaust rendered null and void the promises and covenant of God?"

The answer the pastor gave was a "no"—but a qualified one. No— but we misunderstand the rainbow if we use it as an excuse for our own irresponsibility. God has given us humans freedom, and we must face the real possibility that in our freedom we may bring off the nuclear holocaust that reduces the earth to a shambles.

In the closing two paragraphs, the pastor, adapting King's "dream" language, helped the local congregation actually envision a new (and then relatively unimagined) possibility:

> I have a dream. In my dream the two super-powers find a way to halt the arms race. They do so without naivete, without either giving to the other an undue advantage, without letting themselves be tricked or deceived. And then slowly, a step at a time, they find the way to reduce nuclear arms. They do this, not because they are perfect, not because they have lost all aggressiveness, but because they agree that what is too horrible for God ever to do again is too horrible for humankind to do. Finally the last nuclear weapon is disarmed, and there appears in the sky a great rainbow.
>
> At the foot of that rainbow there really is a pot of gold—billions and billions of dollars now available for economic competition

instead of military competition, available for construction instead of destruction, available to rebuild our decayed and decaying cities, available to make good health care and good education accessible to all people, available as capital for third world development, available to prevent the death of every third child born into this world from starvation and malnutrition.

That would really be a magic bow.[36]

I was present in the congregation the day this sermon was preached, and still remember the sense of empowerment it gave. By painting an alternative world in terms that were also seriously imaginable to that local congregation, the preacher held forth a future that seemed real, palpable, and even attainable. The sermon gave its hearers a world *to live into.* In preaching as local theology, the world-not-yet-imagined breaks in upon the world-as-currently-imagined, and empowering hope is born.

Conclusion

Contextual preaching is an imaginative act of theological construction. The preacher engages his or her own imagination in the hermeneutical task of bringing biblical world and congregational world together in proclamation that is not only faithful to Scripture, but that is also fitting, seriously imaginable, and transformative for the congregation.

In this chapter we have envisioned that interpretive process as a "dance" of the preacher's imagination. The preacher undertakes the dance in partnership with the congregation, Scripture, and church doctrine, allowing contextual concerns to inform the particular shape and ordering of the dance for each occasion of proclamation. The dance style is one that values both textuality and contextuality, both faithfulness to the Gospel and fittingness for the congregation. Thus, the preacher moves from con/text to sermon with fluidity and openness, seeking to discern through the dance a strategy for proclamation that holds these values together in a creative tension.

However, in contextual proclamation the preacher not only functions as dancer, engaging and being engaged in the imaginative act of interpretation. The preacher also functions as choreographer, giving shape and form to the embodied dance for Sunday morning. It is toward the choreography of contextual proclamation—sermonic language and form—that we next turn our attention.

5
Preaching as Folk Art

At its best, Christian preaching is not only an act of theological construction; it is also a work of art. Through its language, images, and form, preaching creates a world and invites the one hearing it to enter it. As Elizabeth Achtemeier asserts, "in the art of preaching, the English language is framed in such a way that the congregation is allowed to enter into a new experience—to exchange their old perceptions of themselves, their world, and God for new perceptions, to step outside an old manner of life and see the possibility of a new one."[1]

Charles Rice says that artistry in the sermon is inescapable because the mystery of divine revelation propels the preacher toward speech which, in some way, reflects that mystery.[2] Preachers, like artists, are engaged in a vocation that requires them to express the inexpressible. Their quest is for symbols which can communicate both the deepest longings of the human spirit, and the deepest mysteries of God and God's revelatory presence in the world. In order to undertake this task, preachers rely upon discipline, imagination, and the illumination of the Spirit.

While agreeing with Achtemeier and Rice that preaching is (at its best) art, it is the particular concern of this book that preaching, given its congregational locus, should also be conceived as *folk art*. Most contemporary authors in the homiletical field speak of the artfulness of proclamation by making reference to the "fine arts." Achtemeier, for example, urges preachers to read fine literature to improve their preaching. Rice encourages pastors to pay greater attention to contemporary literature, plays, and cinema in their proclamation. In homiletics classrooms across the country students are urged to consider the fine arts as prime material for sermon illustrations.

On one level, encouraging such attention to the fine arts is good for preaching. If, as we have suggested, preaching is primarily an act of hermeneutical and artistic imagination, then it is crucial that the preacher feed his or her own imagination in the creative process. Time spent reading a good book or listening to classical music or browsing in an art gallery opens the senses to the mysterious power of art to reveal worlds, and feeds the preacher's own creative and integrative abilities. Fred Craddock, who encourages preachers to read novels, short stories, and poetry at least once a week, reasons:

> Reading good literature enlarges one's capacities as a creative human being and has a cumulative effect on one's vocabulary, use of the language, and powers of imagination. Not by conscious imitation but through the subtle influence of these great storytellers and poets, a preacher becomes more adept at arranging the materials of the sermon so that by restraint and thematic control, interest, clarity, and persuasiveness will be served.[3]

In like manner, the fine arts have proved to be fertile ground for effective sermon illustrations for preachers of generations upon end. Good art is itself able to touch the deep places of the human soul, and to transcend distances of time and space through its symbolic address to the universals of human experience. Through the words of a poet, the preacher is often enabled to express theology far more profoundly than mere prose allows. The skillful preacher can also retell a story or recreate a scene or paint a portrait with words in such a way that even those who are unfamiliar with a particular work of art can become a part of its world, caught up in its mystery.

However, an emphasis upon preaching as "fine art" has also had detrimental effects upon proclamation in our day. Too many pastors have gone into the pulpit on Sunday morning, peppering their sermons with quotations from a favorite novel, citing a beloved poet, or recreating a scene from a contemporary play—only to find that the deep meaning they perceived in these artistic expressions is somehow lost or diminished in their local communities of faith. On a surface level, the art forms themselves may seem far removed from a congregation whose own world more readily revolves around "folk arts" (such as quilting, oral storytelling, banjo-playing), or for whom Broadway and its plays seem as distant as the moon.

On a deeper level, however, lie issues related to congregational subculture and its "thick description" (discussed in chapter 3). Quite often the problem is not only that the preacher is bringing "foreign" materials into the sermon (artistic expressions that are relatively uncommon or not as highly valued in the life of a particular subculture); the difficulty is also that the worldview and values assumed in contemporary or classical art and literature are far removed from the ordinary, everyday worldview and values of a particular faith community. Questions raised about life in a contemporary novel are not the congregation's questions. Assumptions made about God, humanity, nature, and time by the poet are not the congregation's assumptions. Values expressed in a play are at odds with those shared by the congregation, and present a stumbling block for their hearing of the connection the preacher is trying to forge. And so, once again, the sermon lacks in "fittingness." Art, in this instance, opens up a life world—but it is not a world in which local congregants can seriously imagine themselves living and acting.

Preaching as *folk art*, on the other hand, presses toward proclamation that attends as closely to the congregation in its artistic design as it does in its theological construction. The preacher is not only a "local theologian," engaging in a dance of the imagination in order to discern fitting and faithful themes for proclamation. The preacher is also a "folk artist"—searching for the expression of local theology through symbols, forms, and movements that are capable of capturing and transforming the imaginations of a particular local community of faith.

The Preacher as Folk Dancer

While there are many "folk art" forms to which we could liken local preaching (visual art, crafts, literature, poetry, music), my own preferred metaphor for contextual proclamation is that of "folk dance"—especially the circular styles of folk dancing enjoyed by a number of subcultures within the United States.

My exposure to circle dancing came as a child when my family spent several weeks each summer in a retreat center of our denomination in the Blue Ridge mountains of North Carolina. One of the traditions of this community was that on Friday nights everyone gathered at "the barn" for an evening of "big circle mountain dancing." The Stony Creek Boys—a local mountain musical group—brought their banjos and fiddles, and played lively, foot-tapping tunes indigenous to the mountain culture. A local resident, well-acquainted with both the patterns and the practice of the dance, served as our leader.

The leader played many roles at our circle dances. At times he served as dance initiator, standing on the floor with us, grasping the hand of the nearest person, and inviting all—young and old, men and women, partners and singles—to join the circle and become a part of the dance. At times he served as dance modeler, teaching us the steps of the dance not only with his words but also with his bodily motions. At times he served as dance choreographer and caller, directing and giving shape to the dance through his rhyming banter. And, when we totally lost our way and no one got the dance right, he served as corrector and encourager, taking us back to the beginning and patiently walking us through the motions one more time.

One of the great things about big circle mountain dancing was that anyone could join in, and the circle was always open to accommodate one more. Little children could grab the hand of an adult, and be swept along in the tide of the dance. Newcomers, just learning the dance, were always close to someone who knew the steps, and would gladly give instruction. And no one was made to feel they had to get it exactly "right" to participate. Taking part in the dance was always far more important than well-orchestrated steps or precise movements.

Contextual congregational proclamation on Sunday mornings is a lot like folk dance. The preacher, functioning both as dancer and as leader in the dance, stays close to the ground of the local community, inviting and encouraging others to join in the circle dance of faith. The sermon itself is a participatory act in which the preacher models a way of doing theology that meets people where they are, but that also encourages them to stretch themselves by trying new steps, new moves, new patterns of belief and action. In this dance, as in the circle dance, the leader must always be alert to what is happening in the life of the community—sometimes correcting, sometimes encouraging, sometimes guiding, sometimes pushing toward new vistas—as the need arises. And in this dance, as in the circle dance, the preacher is not the only leader. Indeed, there are those in the circle far more adept at the dance than the preacher—faithful Christians who help keep the community growing, learning, and moving in the rhythms of faith by their own seasoned modeling and teaching.

Often we speak of preaching as if it were a performance—akin to a ballet—in which the goal is for everyone in the audience to go away marveling over the skill of the lead performer, the preacher. But when preaching is viewed as folk dance, the goal is quite different: namely, that the leader model the dance of faith in such an accessible, imaginative, earthy, and encouraging way that everyone—young and old, visitor and member, old timer and newcomer—will want to put on his or her own dancing shoes and join in.

The Choreography of Sermon Design

In the last chapter we discussed how the preacher as local theologian prepares for leadership in this dance by first engaging in a dance of his or her own—attending to the rhythms provided by Scripture, congregational subculture, and church traditions in order to discern appropriate themes for proclamation. Now we turn toward the task of creative choreography, asking how the preacher as folk artist can enflesh the sermon's theology in language and form that are equally fitting and transformative for congregational imagination.

The Language of Local Preaching

"Preaching is about the teaching of a new language—the language of Christian faith." "Preaching should be framed in the ordinary language of everyday congregational speech." Out of the tension that exists between these two statements is born the language of the sermon. While preachers do not invent a third amalgamated language in which to preach the gospel, they do, through the bringing together of biblical and congregational vocabularies, name and vision a new reality where gospel and life intersect. Paul Scott Wilson calls this creative and recreative process "language renewal."[4]

For the contextual preacher, language renewal involves both a revisioning of the assumed world of the congregation in light of the language and symbols of the Christian faith, and a reinterpretation of the ancient language of the Christian faith in light of the world of the congregation. Language not only reflects a people's culture; it also has the power to reshape and transform it.

But what does the language of contextual proclamation look like? How might an emphasis upon preaching as "folk art" influence the choices the preacher makes regarding the words, images, and examples used in sermons? While certainly not exhaustive, the following guidelines give initial direction to the preacher who wants to stay closer to the ground of local hearers in the language of proclamation.

1. *Preaching as "folk art" exhibits a preference for the simple, plain, conversational speech of the local congregation.*

When I was in high school I had an English teacher who was fond of saying, "Why use a fifty-cent word when you can use a five-dollar word?" She was, of course, trying to expand our facility with the English language by encouraging us to use words that were more complex and nuanced than our typical teenage vocabularies ordinarily provided.

When preaching is viewed as folk art, however, there are actually very good reasons for choosing a fifty-cent word over a five-dollar word: namely, that some of our five-dollar words may create unnecessary barriers and stumbling blocks for members of our congregations for whom they have little or no meaning.

One of the most consistent complaints that I hear from lay persons about preaching is that sermons are "over our heads." When I ask for elaboration of that phrase, people talk about sermons being too "academic," using too much "theological jargon," assuming more biblical knowledge than they actually have, or using a style of speech that is highly formal and exhibits little humor. (One lay person recently told me that his pastor's idea of "humor" in the pulpit was explicating the difference between two Greek verbs!) By contrast, the people who talk favorably about their preachers often point to their ability to bring the gospel "down to earth" and to communicate it in a way that is clear, appropriately humorous, easy to follow, and interesting.

Preaching as folk art encourages pastors to employ more "folk speech"—the ordinary, everyday, language of local congregations—in their proclamation. The more the preacher can interpret Scripture and its symbols within the particular language of the congregational subculture—employing its peculiar idioms, turns of phrase, colloquialisms, and proverbial sayings—the more "down to earth" the sermon will seem to a local community.

Some years ago Clarence Jordan of the Koinonia Community in Americus, Georgia, published a "Cotton Patch" version of the Gospels, in which he recast stories and sayings of Jesus in the idiom of rural southwest Georgia. Jordan's translations captured the imaginations not only of Georgians, but also of many other readers because of the lively, humorous, and earthy way in which their folk language breathed new life into overly familiar biblical stories.

For example, John the Baptizer was depicted as being dressed in blue jeans and a leather jacket, living on corn bread and collard greens, and "dipping" people in the Chattahoochee.[5] The "God Movement" was compared to a "jeweler looking for special pearls" who, "when he finds a super-duper one . . . goes and unloads his whole stock and buys that pearl." And Judas, after "squealing" on Jesus, told the archbishops and elders that he had "ratted on an innocent man."

Preaching as folk art will search for similar ways to reinterpret Scripture through the language of local speech. Whether it is recasting the Zaccheus story in prison lingo, arguing from the vantage of an upwardly mobile suburbanite with Jesus' injunction to "take no thought for the morrow," or retelling the parable of the laborers in the vineyard from the perspective of a dairy farmer, contextual preaching renews language and faith by its imaginative meeting of the linguistic worlds of biblical text and congregational context.

Theologically, much is at stake here. As long as preachers employ a relatively inaccessible language and style of speech in the pulpit and do not accommodate to the speech of their hearers, they can give the impression: (*a*) that the only true teachers in faith are preachers, or other "learned ones," who have secret knowledge of and access to this holy jargon (thus perpetuating the gnostic heresy); (*b*) that the realm of the sacred is separate and distinct from the realm of the secular, and that it is impossible to speak of the holy in ordinary terms (thus denying the incarnation), or (*c*) that the preacher considers himself or herself to be culturally superior to the hearers, and is only willing to have genuine conversations in faith with those who can speak his or her language (thus denying the call to be servants of a servant Lord).

In preaching as "folk art," on the other hand, the preacher recognizes that the most valuable words (the five-dollar words, if you will) are not those that are the most complex or esoteric, but those that carry the greatest meaning for the hearer. The preacher voluntarily gives up his or her prerogative to use the words she or he may know, in order to use language that the hearer knows. She or he teaches the "language" of faith, but does so in a manner that also engages the everyday language of the hearer.

The goal in striving for such speech is not only that the preacher *avoid* using speech which creates a stumbling block for the hearer. The goal is also that the preacher intentionally *enflesh* the sermon in language which is particular, unique, and "local" in color, so that the gospel message—in its language as well as its theology—becomes incarnate within the real subcultural world its hearers inhabit.

2. *Preaching as folk art uses examples and illustrations that are reflective of life as members of the congregation actually experience it.*

One Sunday, while preaching in a small rural congregation, I used a quotation from theologian Karl Barth in my sermon, giving credit to Barth as I did so. On the way out the door one of my parishioners shook my hand and said, "Well, Nora, you've done some interesting things in your sermons before, but today's sermon took the cake!" "How so?" I asked, dumbfounded (for I thought the sermon had been rather mundane). "Why you've actually started quoting Karl Marx in your preaching!" she replied.

Upon reflection I realized that to my parishioner, the theologian Karl Barth—so much a part of my world—was a remote and totally unknown figure. And so, never having heard of Barth, she made the logical assumption that I must have misspoken the name, and retranslated it into a name with which she was familiar.

Sometimes I fear that we preachers may, on a more regular basis than we would like to admit, fill our sermons with people and situations that seem as remote from our congregations and their contexts as Karl Barth was from this woman's world. For example, I have heard many sermons that hold up as models in faith sports heroes and media stars, or, on the other hand, the Mother Teresas and Martin Luther Kings of the world. While there is nothing wrong with using such examples occasionally, a steady diet of these "larger than life" heroes can be discouraging to local folk who are trying to live their lives faithfully as insurance salespersons, farmers, computer programmers, or high school students. Subtly the message is communicated: the real Christian heroes in life are either martyred, living in India, or have their faces on the cover of a national magazine. (Implied: they are not ordinary folk like us.)

In like manner, there is a temptation in preaching to seek out equally "larger than life" stories and situations with which to illustrate our preaching—the crisis story in which there is a miraculous and extraordinary last-minute intervention by God; the ethical dilemma in which the lines between right and wrong are clearly and easily delineated; the call to obedience that comes as distinctly as handwriting on the wall.

The problem is that for most local folk, everyday life and faith are far less dramatic and more ambiguous than such illustrations suggest. Consequently they hunger for illustrative materials that more accurately reflect life as they actually know and experience it—prayers for miraculous intervention that seem to go unanswered for months on end; ethical dilemmas that are blurred and offer no "happy" solutions; struggles to discern the inscrutable will of God when handwriting on the wall is nowhere apparent.

Preaching as folk art looks for ways to enflesh the gospel in events and people and circumstances that are ordinary and commonplace to the hearers. Rather than aiming for the grandiose, the miraculous, and the extraordinary in illustrative materials, such preaching strives to enflesh the gospel in real-life stories about real-life people in real-life situations with which a local congregation can identify.

Contextual preaching, then, honors local and relatively obscure heroes—the business person whose persistent efforts over many years (and despite numerous obstacles) have finally resulted in the establishment of a community "meals on wheels" program; the retirement home resident whose daily faithfulness and persistence in prayer are an inspiration to others; the teenagers whose alternative drug-and-alcohol-free parties provide an important witness for other youth in the community; a local "Job" whose joy and hope in the face of adversity defy rational explanation. While always taking care not to betray confidences or embarrass local people, preaching as folk art looks for appropriate occasions on which to use examples and illustrations that actually grow out of the life of the congregation or local community in preaching, as well as examples and illustrations from other locales that are "seriously imaginable" within the context of the local congregation.

In like manner, contextual preaching seeks to enflesh large, universal issues and themes in local and particular ways. Global or national justice issues become seriously imaginable when the preacher tells stories about real people whose lives and livelihoods are linked to those issues. Large church bodies become living entities (rather than institutional bureaucracies) when the pastor describes worship at one of their gatherings or tells about the lives of the very local persons who make up their decision-making bodies. Theological terms like "grace" and "righteous anger" take root in local soil when the pastor reminds the parishioners of times when, in their own subcultural worlds, they have encountered undeserved grace in a personal or professional relationship, or have witnessed anger that was genuinely righteous in nature.

In *The Preaching Life* Barbara Brown Taylor labels the preacher a "detective of divinity," whose task it is to search for the extraordinary within the ordinary fabric of everyday existence.

> Day after day I look at my life, the lives of my neighbors, the world in which we all live, and I hunt the hidden figure, the presence that still moves just beneath the surface of every created things. Sometimes I can only make out a hand, or a foot, or an all-seeing eye, but I know it is there, even when I am not able to see it whole.
>
> It is an imaginative enterprise, in which I must first of all give up the notion that I know what I am looking at when I look at the world. I do not know. All I know is that there is always more than meets the eye, and that if I want to see truly, I must be willing to look beyond the appearance of things into the depth of things, into the layers of meaning with which the least blade of grass is endowed.[6]

Preaching as folk art presses pastors to become such detectives of divinity right where they are. Such preaching will not be easily fed by quick-fix pulpit aides that come to pastors unsolicited in the mail, or by books of illustrative materials. Rather, it will require the preacher to do harder, more imaginative work—examining the ordinary world the hearers inhabit, and seeking, like a detective of divinity, to discover the gospel in its midst.

3. Preaching as folk art searches for local images and metaphors capable of bringing the biblical world and the world of the congregation together in transformative ways.

In recent years much has been written about the power of metaphor and image to capture the imaginations of the hearers in preaching. Instead of simply proclaiming an "idea" preachers have been encouraged to search for symbols that can bring congregational world and biblical worlds together in imaginative and transformative ways.

In chapter 4 we said that for the discerning pastor—one who attends in the exegetical process not only to the theological worlds and ideas a biblical text presents, but also to the language through which it does so—the Bible itself offers many transformative symbols for congregational preaching. A boat, threatening to capsize after an unexpected catch of fish at Jesus' command, becomes a metaphor for a congregation reeling from the effects of rapid growth and its resulting tensions.[7] The kingdom of God, envisioned by the prophet Zechariah as a "public park where the streets are safe for children," provides a vision of eschatological hope for a congregation in a city whose streets ordinarily hold terror and death for children.[8] The "river's edge"—where Pharaoh's daughter encounters a Hebrew infant and must decide whether the prejudices and laws of the Egyptians or her own human compassion for this baby will rule her actions—becomes a metaphor for similar decision-making junctures in a congregation's life.[9]

However, preaching as folk art also recognizes that congregations and their day-to-day worlds can also be fertile soil for discovering symbols capable of communicating the gospel in imaginative and transformative ways. Taking a clue from Jesus, whose theological reflection in the Gospels frequently began with some ordinary experience of everyday life (separating wheat from chaff on the threshing floor, traveling from Jerusalem to Jericho, or searching for a lost coin), preaching as folk art uses ordinary local symbols to communicate extraordinary holy truths.

Such preaching will find in a child's experience of the "kitchen"—as a place both of warmth and light and fellowship, and as a place of hard work and service—an appropriate metaphor for the church.[10] Such preaching will discover in the simple practice of "drop line fishing" (versus the more elaborate techniques of "fly fishing") an appropriate metaphor for evangelism as modeled by the disciple Andrew.[11] Such preaching will lift up the daring trust exhibited by junior high youth on a ropes course during a weekend retreat as a metaphor for the kind of risky trust that is required of all Christians in the life of faith.[12] And such preaching will find in a faded and dusty arrangement of wax flowers—painstakingly made for the church by a saint of a previous era—an expression of extravagant devotion, akin to that of the woman who poured costly perfume all over Jesus' feet.[13]

Preaching as folk art does not have to go far afield to find symbols worthy of gospel proclamation. In the ordinary clay of local experience it finds the stuff pots are made of, and uses it to shape earthen vessels capable of conveying the priceless treasures of the gospel.

Forms for Local Preaching

One of the things that perpetually puzzled me during my pastorate among four small churches in central Virginia was that I could take the very same sermon and preach it in each of those churches, and receive markedly different responses from the congregations. Over time, I even began noticing patterns regarding which types of sermons appealed to which congregations.

For example, I nearly always received favorable comments from well-educated members of the two town churches when I preached "doctrinal" sermons—sermons that explained, in a logical and orderly manner, some central theological tenet of the faith. The local school superintendent was especially favorable toward those sermons that deepened his theological understanding of the sacraments.

However, I did not sense that those same doctrinal sermons received nearly as favorable a response from several members of the congregation in a dairy-farming community. Indeed, I became concerned that Lydia, a homemaker with an eighth-grade education and John,[14] a hired laborer on one of the dairy farms, were not altogether able to follow my train of thought in those sermons. The sermons that appealed to them usually contained a great deal more narrative in their structure and a simpler message.

Meanwhile, other members of the dairy-farming community seemed to relish sermons that began with a troublesome issue of life or faith, or with a problematic biblical text, and wrestled with it in a highly inductive manner. When I offered to preach one summer on biblical texts of their choice, members of this congregation consistently requested that I preach on passages that puzzled or troubled them (such as the parable of the vineyard workers who received equal pay for unequal work).

As for the fourth congregation—a very historic church in a rural area—I was intrigued by the fact that every summer when they could invite a preacher of their choice to lead their week of "special services," they inevitably chose someone who preached in a verse-by-verse expository manner. They especially liked preachers who would stand up with nothing but the Bible in their hands, explicating each verse in turn and its meaning for their lives.

The diversity of preferences for sermons and *sermon forms* I encountered in those churches—churches that were all located within a thirty-mile radius of one another—has led me to question the relationship between sermon forms, congregational subcultures, and their "modes of knowing." Are there sermon forms that are more "fitting" and more easily comprehended in one congregational context than in another? Are there clues the pastor can gain, through a closer attending to congregational subculture, that can assist him or her in the construction of sermons that are more "seriously imaginable" for a particular community of faith?

SUBCULTURES AND WAYS OF KNOWING

In recent years the field of homiletics has given considerable attention both to how the shape of diverse biblical literary genres can influence the design of the sermon,[15] and to the significance certain "universal" patterns of human understanding can have for sermon structure.[16] However, considerably less attention has been given to congregational subcultures and the significance their own preferred "ways of knowing and thinking" might have upon the contextual design of sermons.

Yet the reality is that all people don't think alike. There are differences among us and the predominant ways in which we come to knowledge. And some of those differences may well be linked with sociocultural conditions that foster and encourage them.

It is interesting to note, for example, that when Mary Field Belenky and her colleagues undertook their study of women's cognition several years ago, they not only identified five very different "ways of knowing" among the women they interviewed; they also noted significant linkages between those preferred knowledge modes and the sociocultural conditions that fostered them.[17] For example, it was among poor and poorly educated women in the study that Belenky and her colleagues discovered women who were either "silent" knowers (believing themselves incapable of having thoughts worth expressing and thus, virtually having no voice) or "received" knowers (depending upon external authority figures to tell them what to think or believe). Conversely, it was among upper-middle-class, college-educated women that they discovered the "procedural" and "constructed" knowers—women who were not only capable of highly analytic and systematic modes of thought, but who were also capable (especially in the latter category) of integrating intuition and reason in a constructive and critical fashion.

Within and among congregations, then, there are people who come to knowledge in very different ways. The question is, How do we preach "fittingly" amid such diversity? How do preachers stay close to the ground of the hearers in sermon form (as in the theology and language of the sermon) so that local individuals and congregations can best hear and appropriate what we are saying?

LOCAL THEOLOGIES AND LOCAL FORMS

While preaching has not long attended to such matters, those who struggle with the contextualization of theology within diverse cultures around the globe have. One such theologian is Robert Schreiter.

In his book *Constructing Local Theologies* Schreiter argues that theology is not authentically contextual in nature if it attends only to the appropriateness of its themes for the local culture. Genuine local theology must also attend to the fittingness of theological *form* for the context.[18] The theologian should recognize that the very modes in which human beings understand and give expression to their thought are not altogether universal, but are also colored and shaped by the sociocultural contexts out of which they arise.

When Schreiter surveys the world scene, he identifies four different forms local theologies have taken through history, and continue to take in the present day. They are:

1. Theology as *variation on sacred text*—in which the theologian takes a portion of a sacred text (such as a passage from Scripture) and reinterprets its meaning through the signs and symbols of a new culture. Included within this "catch-all" type are: the *commentary* form (giving a verse-by-verse interpretation of a text), the *narrative* form (using a story to extend the text's meaning into the present), and the *anthology* form (in which various discrete portions of the text are linked together to serve some common theme or purpose).

2. Theology as *wisdom*—in which the theologian, who is concerned to integrate all aspects of the seen and unseen world into a unified whole, looks deeply into human experience in order to dis-

cover analogues (or types) of God and God's ordering and sustaining of creation. (This is a common form of theologizing in Eastern Christianity and in a variety of monastic and mystical traditions.)

3. Theology as *sure knowledge*—in which the theologian is concerned to give as exact and critical account of the Christian faith in relation to contemporary reality as possible. (Sure knowledge is the predominant form of theologizing among Western systematic and apologetic theologians.)

4. Theology as *praxis*—that aims to transform false and oppressive social relationships by naming and critiquing them, strategizing for transformative action, and critically reflecting upon that action. (Praxis modes of theologizing are evidenced among many of the world's liberation theologies.)

Schreiter not only identifies the forms, however. He also makes connections between the forms and the diverse cultural conditions that seem to foster each of them.

For example, *variation on sacred text* theology tends to flourish in cultures that are primarily oral (as opposed to literate) and in which the sacred text itself has an assumed authority and is relatively protected from outside challenges and threats. *Wisdom* theology arises out of cultures where there is a sense of cosmic unity between human beings and all things seen and unseen, where strong emphasis is placed on personal growth through deepened interiority, where people value wisdom more than learning or wealth, and where the culture itself (being less pluralistic) is more hospitable to a unified worldview. By contrast, *sure knowledge* theology tends to flourish either in highly specialized and differentiated urban economies, or in cultures where there is a plurality of competing worldviews. And *praxis* theology finds fertile soil in cultures where people are struggling to break free from oppression.

THEOLOGICAL FORMS AND PREACHING FORMS

Although Schreiter locates all preaching under one subset of one theological type (the commentary form), I do not think it takes a great deal of imagination to identify sermon forms which might be considered analogous to all four of Schreiter's theological types. For example, "variation on sacred text" forms are suggestive of homiletical structures as diverse as the verse-by-verse expository sermon form (paralleling the "commentary" form), various styles of narrative preaching (paralleling the "story" form), and the Billy Graham "anthology" style of preaching (in which discrete Bible verses are linked together around a central theme or topic).

"Sure knowledge" preaching, on the other hand, finds parallels in classic deductive sermon forms (in which the preacher begins with affirmation of a general theological truth and then fleshes out its meaning for life in several points) or in forms which give an ordered and systematic defense or accounting of the faith (such as in "apologetic" or "doctrinal" preaching).

"Wisdom" preaching, by contrast, tends to find its analogues on the inductive side of the form spectrum, in structures that begin with life's questions or tensions, and then take the hearers on a quest for truth; in sermons that plunge deeply into the interiority of Christian experience in order to find analogs for God and God's ways with the world; or in sermons that create a sense of unity and wholeness between things that are frequently disconnected.

Finally, "praxis" (or "liberation") preaching is marked by its critique of the forces of oppression in contemporary life and its movement toward liberating action in the world. Such preaching often moves from analysis of the current social order and its injustices, to the gospel's liberating message, to a call for a response that engages not only the mind and heart, but also the will and the body.

The more complex question is, Are there linkages (analogous to those Schreiter identifies) that can also be observed between sermon forms and congregational subcultures that foster or encourage them? Are there sermon forms which are more likely to arise out of and to flourish within one congregational context than in another? My own hunch (based not on formal research, but on informal observation of preaching and its contexts) is that there may well be.

For example, it was within the two rural (and more isolated) churches that I served that preferences were most often expressed for "variation on sacred text" forms. In the dairy-farming community, the expressed desire—especially among less-educated members—was for more storytelling in proclamation; in the historic congregation, the preference was for more expository preaching. Yet both congregations exhibited the two cultural conditions Schreiter identifies as being favorable for fostering "variation on sacred text" forms.

First, both were contexts in which the Bible itself had a certain assumed authority and was still relatively protected from outside threats. On the whole, people in these churches did not question the Bible's authority; they assumed it. They were far more interested in plumbing the depths of biblical texts through study and preaching, than in debating whether or not this sacred text had any meaning for their lives.

Second, to a certain degree in both communities—but especially in the dairy-farming community—I experienced cultures in which "orality" still held sway over literacy. Visiting and storytelling were still primary forms of entertainment in this rural area. Further, whenever I asked a direct question in this congregation—regardless of the context—I usually received in reply an indirect response, communicated in story form.

I would also note that this same dairy-farming community, which regularly expressed appreciation for my own inductive tendencies in preaching, mirrored many of the sociocultural conditions Schreiter associates with a "wisdom" orientation. In this church the members lived in harmony with the cycles of the seasons and seemed to have a deep sense of their own place within the cosmos. Wisdom was far more highly valued than either wealth or "book learning," and great authority was vested in those the community deemed to be sages.

By way of contrast, it was among the more "cosmopolitan" members of the town churches—members who had travelled more widely and who were more attuned to the competing worldviews of a pluralistic culture—that the greatest appreciation for "sure knowledge" preaching was expressed.

WAYS OF KNOWING AND FORMS OF PREACHING

Now I do not want to imply, through these observations, that a one-to-one correlation exists between congregational sermon form preferences and subcultural ways of knowing. Preaching is far too complicated and mysterious an act to reduce it to such simple formulas.

Nor do I want to imply that congregations are monolithic in their "ways of knowing." Within any given congregation on a Sunday morning there are likely to be people present who have a diversity of knowing modes. Factors other than subculture—such as age, gender, the congregation's capacity for "ambiguity" or their experience with past preachers—can also influence cognitive styles and sermon form preferences within a community of faith.

Finally, I am not suggesting that subcultural ways of knowing should be the sole determinative factor in regard to sermon form. Sermon form, like sermon content, is born out of a dance of the imagination that engages many partners—including the shape of the biblical text and more universal modes of human understanding. Indeed, for the contextual preacher, form and content are inextricably linked.

However, what I do want to suggest is that congregational "ways of knowing" ought to be one factor the contextual preacher considers in the design of the sermon. The following guidelines can assist the preacher who seeks to be a "folk artist"—not only in relation to the language of the sermon, but also in considering its form.

1. *When sermons seem to be "missing" local congregations, the preacher as folk artist needs to ask, Could form be a part of the problem?*

A pastor (we'll call her Carol) recently told me of her experience of preaching a Christmas Eve communion meditation in two different congregations that she had served. The sermon is brief and beautifully written, capturing the mystery and wonder of that first holy night in a style that is highly poetic—both in language and in form. It is a work of art.

Carol first prepared and preached this sermon several years ago for a large, well-educated urban congregation in the South which she was then serving as an associate pastor. The congregation—which has a love for the fine arts (and frequently offers organ recitals, art exhibits, or classes on theology and literature in its downtown Gothic edifice)—loved her sermon. "They couldn't say enough good about it," she reports.

This past Christmas Eve Carol again preached her poetic meditation—this time in the small Northeastern town where she pastors a predominantly blue-collar congregation. The response, she reports, was vastly different. Not only was the immediate congregational response to the sermon underwhelming. Most astonishing was the fact that several members of the worship committee (who had been present for the service) commented at their next meeting that they hoped next year's Christmas Eve service—as opposed to this year's— would actually include a sermon!

Now what is going on here? Why does one congregation respond so positively to a sermon that the next has difficulty hearing at all? I strongly suspect that at least in part, the issue is one of form. A sermon form that was genuinely "folk art" of the highest order in Carol's first congregation, comes across to the second as the "fine art" of an alien culture. Indeed, so removed is this form and its way of knowing from the second congregation's everyday subcultural world (including, I would suspect, their past experience of preaching) that many don't even recognize the sermon to be a sermon.

When preachers sense that sermons are "missing" their congregations, one of the questions they should ask is, Could it be that the form of the sermon—and its assumed way of knowing—is a part of the problem? A first step toward removing "false stumbling blocks" in preaching is to recognize where they lie.

2. Preaching as folk art avoids the consistent use of sermon forms that deny or devalue the predominant local and subcultural modes of knowing within a congregation.

It is one thing for the creative pastor to occasionally preach a sermon that "misses" a local congregation through its use of a novel form. It is quite another for the pastor to consistently preach in structures that demean or devalue the predominant ways in which a local congregation comes to deeper knowledge in faith. To preach a steady diet of "sure knowledge" sermons in a community more attuned to "narrative" modes of theologizing, or to deliver a steady diet of "wisdom" sermons in a community with a "praxis" orientation not only can evidence insensitivity on the part of the pastor; such sermons can also become, over time, demoralizing for the hearers.

One of the reasons Schreiter believes it is critical for theologians to attend to culture in the matter of form is that without such attention, the theologian may be in danger of promoting "false consciousness"—implicitly teaching people that their own ways of coming to knowledge and of expressing faith are inadequate or inappropriate. My own sense of the relative inaccessibility of my "sure knowledge" (doctrinal) sermons to Lydia and John and other members of my first parish convinces me that his point is worthy of the preacher's consideration. To consistently preach in a manner that denies the ways local people come to knowledge—especially a poorer or less well educated people—is not only an affront to them; it is also an affront to the gospel of Christ with its bias toward "the least of these."

Preaching as folk art, then, will attend carefully to congregations and the ways in which they express their own faith. The preacher will avoid the sustained use of sermon forms that create "false stumbling blocks" and prohibit a full and intelligible hearing of the gospel message. More positively, preachers will seek to honor, through their sermon structures, the ways in which local people actually come to knowledge of, and give expression to, their own faith.

3. *Preaching as folk art encourages experimentation in sermon form.*

Just as there is a diversity of legitimate forms that local theologizing can take on the global scene, so there is a diversity of legitimate forms that preaching can take within congregational subcultures. There is no "one right way" for biblical world and congregational world to meet in sermonic form. Indeed, the very meeting of the two worlds creates new and exciting possibilities for the preacher's craft as folk artist.

The contextual preacher opens himself or herself to the imaginative possibilities such an encounter can afford. Rather than taking a tried and true sermon form and using it—like a mold—to give shape and form to proclamation, preaching as folk art allows form itself to emerge out of the unique meeting of text and context. There is "play" in the process, as the preacher seeks to craft a form that is both fitting and transformative.

At times the text itself will suggest a form for preaching. The story of Jacob's wrestling at the Jabbok, for example, provides a structure through which the congregation can reflect upon its own times of wrestling with God, receiving a blessing, and leaving the encounter with a limp. The contrast in Revelation 5—between the powerful lion who is expected to unfurl the scroll that reveals the destiny of human history, and the weak and bleeding lamb who is actually deemed worthy—provides two tensive poles around which to structure a sermon on the nature of the church, its temptations (to exert power like a lion), and its calling (to follow the lamb's way of suffering love) in today's world.

Yet at other times, the sermon may take more of its formal cues from congregational context. A sermon, preached on the occasion of the infant baptism of a fourth-generation church member in a historical congregation, takes the form of a letter that is to be read to the infant some years hence. A sermon, preached on Palm Sunday in a small country church full of children waving palm branches, becomes a narrative account of that first happy/sad palm parade, as told from the vantage of a child. While yet another sermon, preached on Christmas Eve in a highly literate congregation, strives through poetry to express the unfathomable mystery of the Word become flesh.

In contextual proclamation experimentation in form is not undertaken for the sake of novelty or even for the sake of keeping closer to the structural intent of the biblical text. Rather, it is undertaken toward the end of crafting sermons, the form of whose content is also "fitting" for a local community of faith.

4. Preaching as folk art sometimes uses form itself to stretch and expand the horizons of congregational understanding.

In form, as well as in content and language, contextual preaching has transformative power. It has the potential not only to meet people where they are, but also to stretch and expand their own ways of knowing God. While preachers as folk artists will want to avoid using forms that consistently deny or devalue valid "ways of knowing" in congregational life and (positively) to preach in structures that are accessible to their hearers, they will also recognize the potential form has to stretch or expand congregational understanding. In contextual proclamation, fittingness in form (as in language and theology) never simply means giving people what they want.

Consider, for example, the congregant who is a "received" knower (according to Belenky's framework), depending largely upon outside authorities to instruct her in the ways of truth. Although she may actually prefer sermons (and sermon forms) that tell her deductively and definitively what to believe, a steady diet of such preaching could actually discourage her even further from making her own discoveries of faith, or from trusting her own theological voice. By contrast, sermons that begin with questions (not answers) and that leave her some freedom to make her own theological decisions, may become vehicles of transformative power.

Or consider a congregation that loves verse-by-verse expository preaching, but that also has tendencies toward bibliolatry. To regularly give this community of faith what it desires in sermon form may not actually be in its best theological interest. By contrast, the intentional use of other (equally accessible) sermon structures can open new vistas for congregational understanding of the Bible itself, and of the diverse ways its gospel can be interpreted in proclamation.

Preaching as folk art has potential not only to influence *what* people think, but also *how* they think. Greater attention to congregational modes of knowing can assist the preacher in shaping sermons that are not only more seriously imaginable for a local community of faith, but that are also more transformative for the ways in which people come to know and express their own faith.

Conclusion

In the circle dance of preaching, the pastor as folk artist not only stays close to the pulse of the local congregation in discerning what to preach; the pastor also stays close to local rhythms in discerning how to give appropriate language and form to the sermon. Attending carefully to the congregation's own idiom and ways of knowing, the pastor designs sermonic choreography that is accessible yet also stretching, affirming yet also challenging, fitting yet also transformative.

Certainly it is the Spirit that ultimately provides the music for this dance of faith. And it is the Spirit that must move if the dancers (including the preacher) are to be inspired, energized, and empowered for the dance.

Yet I am also convinced that preachers can be better instruments of the Spirit in this process. By attending closely to congregations and their cultures, by identifying and removing false stumbling blocks to the hearing of the gospel, and by enfleshing the gospel in sermons which are—in their theology, language, and form—both more fitting and more transformative for local communities of faith, preachers encourage others to join the circle and to participate with their whole beings in the gospel's liberating dance.

PASTOR, LEAD OUR CIRCLE DANCE

Pastor, lead our circle dance
which the Spirit has begun.
Help us hand in hand advance,
show us how to move as one.
Some demand a driving beat,
others ask to slow the pace.
Teach us how to bend and meet
our conflicted needs with grace.

From the center lead and show
steps and leaps we never tried,
then allow the dance to flow,
dancing with us side by side.
Let each dancer take a turn,
dancing in the center free
so that all can teach and learn
what our circle dance could be.

If the circle gets too tight
stop the dance and don't begin
till our open hands invite
all whom Jesus welcomes in.
For the dance of faith belongs
to the strangers in the street,
and we need their steps and songs
for the dance to be complete.

Pastor, lead our circle dance
as the Spirit leads and calls
till the circle's whole expanse
moves beyond our bounds and walls
and we dance with distant suns
dancing in the dark above,
dancing as creation runs
on the energies of love.

Poem by Thomas H. Troeger, *Borrowed Light: Hymn Texts, Prayers, Poems* (New York: Oxford University Press, 1994), 64. Reprinted by permission.

Notes

Chapter 1. The Culture Shock of Preaching

1. A 1980 study by sociologists Hart M. Nelson and Mary Ann Maguire indicated that one of the dilemmas facing mainline denominations is that most of their clergy come from and have a proclivity to speak to the world-view of urban cosmopolitans rather than that of rural, small town people. Hart M. Nelson and Mary Ann Maguire, "The Two Worlds of Clergy and Congregation: Dilemma for Mainline Denominations," *Sociological Analysis* (Spring 1980), 74.

2. Wade Clark Roof, *Community and Commitment: Religious Plausibility in a Liberal Protestant Church* (New York: Elsevier, 1978).

3. Roy M. Oswald, *Crossing the Boundary between Seminary and Parish* (Washington, D.C.: The Alban Institute, 1979), 11.

4. Leander E. Keck, *The Bible in the Pulpit: The Renewal of Biblical Preaching* (Nashville: Abingdon, 1978), 62.

5. Clyde Kluckhohn and Henry Murray, *Personality in Nature, Society, and Culture* (New York: Alfred A. Knopf, 1948).

6. Clifford Geertz, *The Interpretation of Cultures* (New York: Basic Books, 1973), 89.

7. Christian educator Denham Grierson says that every congregation is also, in certain respects, like all others, like some others, and like no others. *Transforming a People of God* (Melbourne: The Joint Board of Christian Education of Australia and New Zealand, 1984), 16–18.

8. In the *Encyclopedia of Anthropology*, ed. David E. Hunter and Phillip Whitten (New York: Harper & Row, 1976), "subculture" is defined as "a group within a society which shares the fundamental values of the society but which also has its own distinctive folkways, mores, values, and lifestyles" (374).

9. See Marvin Harris, *Cultural Anthropology* (New York: Harper & Row, 1983), 6.

10. H. Richard Niebuhr, *The Social Sources of Denominationalism* (New York: Henry Holt, 1929).

11. Wade Clark Roof and William McKinney, *American Mainline Religion: Its Changing Shape and Future* (New Brunswick: Rutgers University Press, 1987), 106–47.

12. Ibid., 69.

13. C. Ellis Nelson, *Where Faith Begins* (Richmond: John Knox, 1967), 183.

14. Ibid., 186.

15. James F. Hopewell, *Congregation: Stories and Structures*, ed. Barbara G. Wheeler (Philadelphia: Fortress Press, 1987), 3–18.

16. Ibid., 5.

17. Ibid., 55–192.

18. See Richard E. Porter and Larry A. Samovar, "Approaching Intercultural Communication," in *Intercultural Communication: A Reader*, 5th ed. (Belmont, Calif.: Wadsworth, 1988), 15–30; and L. E. Sarbaugh, *Intercultural Communication*, rev. ed. (New Brunswick: Transaction Books, 1988).

19. Sarbaugh, *Intercultural Communication*, 24–46.

20. Studies in the intercultural communications field suggest that the following personality traits can increase the pastor's potential for reacculturation and for effective communication in a new setting: empathy, flexibility, the capacity to communicate respect and be nonjudgmental, the ability to personalize one's knowledge and perceptions, and tolerance for ambiguity. See Brent D. Ruben, "Human Communication and Cross-Cultural Effectiveness," in *Intercultural Communication*, 338–46.

21. St. Augustine, *The First Catechetical Instruction (De Catechizondis Rudibus)* in *Ancient Christian Writers*, No. 2, trans. and annotated by Joseph P. Christopher (Westminster, Md.: Newman Bookshop, 1946), 50.

22. David Buttrick, *Homiletic: Moves and Structures* (Philadelphia: Fortress Press, 1987). Buttrick gave this definition of "consciousness" during a question and answer session at a meeting of the Academy of Homiletics, Drew University, Madison, N.J., in December, 1988. He also uses the term "awareness" interchangeably with "consciousness" in his text.

23. Ibid., 274.

24. Ibid., 443–44.

25. J. Randall Nichols, *Building the Word: The Dynamics of Communication and Preaching* (San Francisco: Harper & Row, 1980), 7–12.

26. See Robert N. Bellah, Richard Madsen, William M. Sullivan, Ann Swidler, and Steven M. Tipton, *Habits of the Heart: Individualism and Commitment in American Life* (Berkeley and Los Angeles: University of California Press, 1985).

27. Henry H. Mitchell, *Black Preaching* (San Francisco: Harper & Row, 1979).

28. Henry H. Mitchell, *The Recovery of Preaching* (San Francisco: Harper & Row, 1977).

29. Ibid., 24.

30. Ibid., 11.

31. Ibid., 29.

32. Arthur Van Seters, ed., *Preaching as a Social Act: Theology and Practice* (Nashville: Abingdon, 1988).

33. Walter Brueggemann, "The Social Nature of the Biblical Text for Preaching," in Van Seters, ed., *Preaching as a Social Act*, 128.

34. Don M. Wardlaw, "Preaching as the Interface of Two Social Worlds: The Congregation as Corporate Agent in the Act of Preaching," in Van Seters, ed., *Preaching as a Social Act*, 55–93.

35. Edwina Hunter, "The Preacher as a Social Being in the Community of Faith," in Van Seters, ed., *Preaching as a Social Act*, 95–125.

36. Thomas G. Long, *The Witness of Preaching* (Louisville: Westminster/ John Knox, 1989), 79.

37. Ibid., 70.

38. Ibid., 78–91.

39. Ibid., 175–77.

40. "The more honest we are with ourselves about our own lives—the places of strength and trust, the crevices of doubt, the moments of kindness, the hidden cruelties—the more we find ourselves on common ground with the others who will hear the sermon." Ibid., 55. Long's discussion of "An Awareness of the Circumstances of the Hearers" occurs on pp. 55–57 in a chapter entitled "The Biblical Witness in Preaching."

41. Ibid., 60–77.

42. Fred B. Craddock, *Preaching* (Nashville: Abingdon Press, 1985), 92.

43. Ibid., 85.

44. Ibid., 98.

45. Ibid., 93–98.

46. Ibid., 95.

47. Craddock warns, however, that neither being a pastor nor serving long years in the parish insures that a person will have a well-developed capacity for empathetic imagination. He encourages development of this gift through listening, observation, and reading the insights of other observers of human behavior. Ibid., 96–97.

48. Ibid., 95.

49. Ibid., 91.

50. For a brief overview of the history and development of the field of "congregational studies," see Allison Stokes and David A. Roozen, "The Unfolding Story of Congregational Studies," in *Carriers of Faith: Lessons from Congregational Studies*, ed. Carl S. Dudley, Jackson W. Carroll, and James P. Wind (Louisville: Westminster/John Knox, 1991), 183–92.

For helpful and comprehensive bibliographies of extant works in congregational studies see: Carl Dudley and James Hopewell, "Understanding and Activating Congregations," in Carl S. Dudley, ed., *Building Effective Ministry: Theory and Practice in the Local Church* (San Francisco: Harper & Row, 1983), 246–56. See also endnotes for chap. 2, Hopewell, *Congregation*, 46–47.

51. Jackson W. Carroll, Carl S. Dudley, and William McKinney, eds., *Handbook for Congregational Studies* (Nashville: Abingdon, 1986), 11–15.

52. Craddock, *Preaching*, 98.

Chapter 2. Aiming toward Contextual Preaching

1. Stephen B. Bevans, *Models of Contextual Theology* (Maryknoll, N.Y.: Orbis, 1992), xiii.

2. Ibid. Italics added for emphasis.

3. Ibid., 1.

4. Acts 2:7b-8 (New Revised Standard Version).

5. Paul Tillich, *Theology of Culture*, ed. Robert C. Kimball (New York: Oxford University Press, 1959), 201.

6. Ibid.

7. Ibid., 213.

8. See John H. Leith, *Introduction to the Reformed Tradition* (Atlanta: John Knox, 1977), 80–81. See also his article "Reformed Preaching Today," *Princeton Seminary Bulletin* 10, no. 3 (1989): 224–57.

9. John H. Leith quotes Ford Lewis Battles in "Calvin's Doctrine of the Proclamation of the Word and its Significance for Today in Light of Recent Research," unpublished paper presented to Calvin Studies Colloquium, 64.

10. For this discussion I am indebted to Ford Lewis Battles, "God Was Accommodating Himself to Human Capacity," *Readings in Calvin's Theology*, ed. Donald J. McKim (Grand Rapids: Baker, 1984), 21–42.

11. Ibid., 36. The Latin term *captus* means "capacity" or "power of comprehension."

12. Ibid., 22.

13. From Calvin's *Commentary on 1 Peter* (1:20) as quoted in ibid., 42.

14. From Calvin's *Institutes of the Christian Religion* 4.17.5, as quoted in ibid., 4.

15. Clyde Fant, *Bonhoeffer: Worldly Preaching* (Nashville: Thomas J. Nelson, 1975), 126.

16. Ibid., 127.

17. Walter Brueggemann, "The Social Nature of the Biblical Text for Preaching," in *Preaching as a Social Act*, ed. Arthur Van Seters (Nashville: Abingdon, 1988), 126.

18. I am indebted to theologian Robert J. Schreiter both for the term "local theology" and for his own very helpful discussion regarding the "construction of local theologies" on a global basis. His thinking has greatly informed my own. See Schreiter, *Constructing Local Theologies* (Maryknoll, N.Y.: Orbis, 1985).

19. See Ernesto Cardenal, *The Gospel in Solentiname*, Vol. 3 (Maryknoll, N.Y.: Orbis, 1979), trans. Donald D. Walsh, for an example of "local theology" that emerged from a congregation of Nicaraguan farm workers.

20. Neill Q. Hamilton, "Friday Morning Comments on the Handbook," correspondence with the editors as quoted in *Handbook for Congregational Studies*, ed. Jackson W. Carroll, Carl S. Dudley, William McKinney (Nashville: Abingdon, 1986), 19. Emphasis added.

21. Edmund A. Steimle, Morris J. Niedenthal, and Charles L. Rice, eds., *Preaching the Story* (Philadelphia: Fortress Press, 1980), 168–69.

22. Fred B. Craddock, *Preaching* (Nashville: Abingdon Press, 1985), 91–92. Emphasis added.

23. Ibid., 26.

24. Ibid., 27.

25. M. M. Thomas, *Toward a Theology of Contemporary Ecumenism: A Collection of Addresses to Ecumenical Gatherings (1947–1975)* (Madras, India: The Christian Literature Society, 1978), 24. Thomas's address, here republished, was first published in the *Student World* (Fourth Quarter 1950) under the title "An Irrelevant Profession?"

26. Ibid., 25.

27. David H. Kelsey, *The Uses of Scripture in Recent Theology* (Philadelphia: Fortress Press, 1975), 170–74.

28. Ibid., 172.

29. Ibid., 172–73.

30. Ibid., 173.

31. See Robert Schreiter, *Constructing Local Theologies*, 59–60; and Charles H. Kraft, *Christianity in Culture: A Study in Dynamic Biblical Theologizing in Cross-Cultural Perspective* (Maryknoll, N.Y.: Orbis, 1984), 147–66.

32. St. Augustine, *On Christian Doctrine*, D. W. Robertson, Jr, trans. (Indianapolis: Bobbs-Merrill Educational Publishing, 1958), 142.

33. Garrett Green, *Imagining God: Theology and the Religious Imagination* (San Francisco: Harper & Row, 1989), 40.

34. See Pss. 14:1 and 53:1 for instances of the "heart" functioning as the seat of intellect, and Lam. 2:11 for an instance of the heart as an emotional center.

35. Green, *Imagining God*, 149.

36. Ibid.

37. Louis Luzbetak, "Signs of Progress in Contextual Methodology," *Verbum svd* 22 (1981): 39.

38. Walter Brueggemann, "The Preacher, Text, and People," *Theology Today* 47 (October 1990): 237–47. Brueggemann adopts the concept of "triangling" from family therapists Murray Bowen, *Family Therapy in Clinical Practice* (New York: J. Aranson, 1978), and Edwin H. Friedman, *Generation to Generation: Family Process in Church and Synagogue* (New York: Guilford Press, 1985).

39. Schreiter, *Constructing Local Theologies*, 20.

40. Ibid., 58.

41. Ibid., 16–19.

42. See Walter Brueggemann, *The Prophetic Imagination* (Philadelphia: Fortress Press, 1978), especially pp. 44–61.

Chapter 3. Exegeting the Congregation

1. Charles V. Gerkin, *Widening the Horizons: Pastoral Responses to a Fragmented Society* (Philadelphia: Westminster, 1988), 61. Gerkin adopts the phrase "fusions of horizons" from philosopher Hans-Georg Gadamer and the phrase "worlds of meaning" from philosopher Paul Ricoeur.

2. "Semiotic" comes from the Greek *semeion*, meaning "sign" or "symbol." While the term is common in many academic circles, it carries little meaning for most pastors and lay persons of my acquaintance. Thus, I have opted to use the more accessible and readily intelligible term *symbolic* in my discussion of cultural anthropology and congregational exegesis.

3. See prior discussion of the four entry points for analyzing congregations—program, process, social context, and identity—in chap. 1, p. 29.

4. Clifford Geertz, *The Interpretation of Cultures* (New York: Basic Books, 1973), 3–30.

5. Anthropologist Bronislaw Malinowski originated "participant-observation" as a field method, insisting that ethnographers become immersed in

the day-to-day activities of the culture being studied, learning to speak the language of its people and actually living among them. Such participation allowed the ethnographer to record the behaviors of a people under a variety of circumstances, and also helped to minimize the effect of the ethnographer's own presence upon the people's responses. See Bronislaw Malinowski, *Argonauts of the Western Pacific* (New York: Dutton, 1961).

6. Clifford Geertz cites this example of Gilbert Ryle in *The Interpretation of Cultures*, 6–7.

7. Ibid., 15.

8. Ibid., 24.

9. Denham Grierson, *Transforming a People of God* (Melbourne: The Joint Board of Christian Education of Australia and New Zealand, 1984), 43.

10. For a fuller discussion of "insiders" and "outsiders," see chap. 2, pp. 49–53.

11. For a fuller discussion of "culture texts" see B. A. Uspenskij et al., "Theses on the Semiotic Study of Cultures (As Applied to Slavic Texts)," *Structure of Texts and Semiotics of Culture*, ed. Jan Van Der Eng and Mojmir Grygar (The Hague and Paris: Mouton, 1973), 1–28.

12. Robert Schreiter, *Constructing Local Theologies* (Maryknoll, N.Y.: Orbis, 1985), 62.

13. See James Hopewell, *Congregation: Stories and Structures*, ed. Barbara G. Wheeler (Philadelphia: Fortress Press, 1987).

14. Ibid.

15. James Clifton, "Ethnography," in *Encyclopedia of Anthropology*, ed. David E. Hunter and Phillip Whitten (New York: Harper & Row, 1976), 148.

16. All of the questions except "What has happened that has pleased you?" are recommended in *Handbook for Congregational Studies*, ed. Jackson W. Carroll, Carl S. Dudley, and William McKinney (Nashville: Abingdon, 1986), 24.

17. Ibid., 24–25.

18. James Wind, *Places of Worship: Exploring Their History*, "The Nearby History Series," vol. 4, ed. David E. Kyvig and Myron A. Marty (Nashville: American Association for State and Local History, 1990), 58–63.

19. Carroll et al., *Handbook for Congregational Studies*, 44.

20. Wind, *Places of Worship*, 52–61.

21. Carroll et al., *Handbook for Congregational Studies*, 43.

22. Douglas A. Walrath, "Types of Small Congregations and Their Implications for Planning," *Small Churches Are Beautiful*, ed. Jackson W. Carroll (San Francisco: Harper & Row, 1977), 33–61. The twelve congregational

types Walrath identifies are: Midtown, Inner City, Inner-Urban, Outer-Urban, City Suburb, Metropolitan Suburb, Fringe Suburb, Fringe Village, Fringe Settlement, Independent City, Rural Village, and Rural Settlement.

23. Wind says, "At best, buildings provide clues about a congregation at certain key moments in its life—at the time of its founding or the time of a move to a new location, or the time when sufficient dis-ease about an old architectural or artistic style existed to motivate a congregation to rearrange the furniture or redesign its home." *Places of Worship*, 9.

24. Ibid.

25. Carroll et al., *Handbook for Congregational Studies*, 37.

26. Victor Turner and Edith Turner, *Image and Pilgrimage in Christian Culture: Anthropological Perspectives* (New York: Columbia University Press, 1978), 244.

27. Stewart Guthrie, "Ritual," in *Encyclopedia of Anthropology*, David E. Hunter and Phillip Whitten, eds. (New York: Harper & Row, 1976), 336–37.

28. Marvin Harris, *Cultural Anthropology* (New York: Harper & Row, 1983), 202. Anthropologist Arnold van Gennep was actually the first to identify and categorize "rites of passage" in *The Rites of Passage* (Chicago: University of Chicago Press, 1960 [first published in 1909]). For an early discussion of "rites of intensification," see Eliot D. Chapple and Carleton Coon, *Principles of Anthropology* (New York: Holt, Rinehart & Winston, 1942).

29. Harris, *Cultural Anthropology*, 202.

30. The terms "dramatic unity" and "ritual symbol" are used and defined by Victor and Edith Turner in *Image and Pilgrimage in Christian Culture*, 243–44.

31. Geertz, *Interpretation of Cultures*, 17.

32. Robert Schreiter maintains that one significant way to discern how identity is structured in a culture is by identifying the invisible boundaries and boundary markers that separate "us" from "not-us." See *Constructing Local Theologies*, 63–67.

33. Clifford Geertz defines "worldview" as a people's "picture of the way things in sheer actuality are, their concept of nature, of self, of society." *Interpretation of Cultures*, 127.

34. Ibid.

35. Robert Redfield, *The Primitive World and Its Transformations* (Ithaca, N.Y.: Cornell University Press, 1953), 87.

36. Ibid., 96.

37. Ibid., 90–104.

38. Florence Rockwood Kluckhohn and Fred L. Strodtbeck define "value-orientations" as "complex but definitely patterned (rank-ordered) principles, resulting from the transactional interplay of three analytically distinguishable elements of the evaluative process—the cognitive, the affective, and the directive elements—which give order and direction to the ever-flowing stream of human acts and thoughts as these relate to the solution of 'common human' problems." *Variations in Value Orientations* (Evanston, Ill. and Elmsford, N.Y.: Row, Peterson, 1961), 4.

39. Ibid., 10–19.

40. In *Models of the Church* (Garden City, N.Y.: Image Books, A Division of Doubleday, 1978) Roman Catholic theologian Avery Dulles identified five models of the church: institution, mystical communion, sacrament, herald, and servant. The terms I use here are adaptations of Dulles's categories, as used by Protestant and Reformed theologian Daniel L. Migliore, *Faith Seeking Understanding* (Grand Rapids, Mich.: Wm. B. Eerdmans, 1991), 192–200.

41. See H. Richard Niebuhr, *Christ and Culture* (New York: Harper & Row, 1951). See also William J. Carl III, *Preaching Christian Doctrine* (Philadelphia: Fortress Press, 1984), 126–34, for a discussion of how a preacher's own stance in relation to Niebuhr's categories can affect his or her proclamation.

42. For a fuller discussion of these missional orientations, see David A. Roozen, William McKinney, and Jackson W. Carroll, *Varieties of Religious Presence: Mission in Public Life* (New York: Pilgrim, 1984).

43. Carl S. Dudley and Sally A. Johnson, "Congregational Self-Images for Social Ministry," in *Carriers of Faith: Lessons from Congregational Studies*, ed. Carl S. Dudley, Jackson W. Carroll, and James P. Wind (Louisville: Westminster/John Knox, 1991), 104–21.

44. See James Hopewell, *Congregation*, 55–100, and also his summary in Carroll et al., *Handbook for Congregational Studies*, 33–35. In the Appendix to *Congregation*, 203–11, Hopewell provides a "World View Test" that can be utilized with congregation members to check worldview perceptions gained by other means.

45. Hopewell, *Congregation*, 105–06.

46. Ibid., 114.

47. Ibid., 111–12.

48. Hopewell actually opposes using biblical stories as congregational analogues on the grounds that (1) biblical stories are such standard fare for most congregations that they rarely awaken a fresh self-understanding, and

(2) using biblical stories as analogues for congregational character is a misappropriation of texts that are intended to sound a prophetic and challenging word in relation to the congregational self-understanding (ibid., 113–14).

By contrast I would argue that (1) it is the very accessibility of biblical stories to diverse subcultural congregations that make them attractive as analogues for congregational understanding; (2) biblical stories are not nearly as well known in congregational life as we might wish, and such a use of these stories can also further the cause of biblical literacy; and (3) it is the very prophetic nature of biblical texts—their ability not only to tell us who we are but to offer hope and challenge for what we can become—that make them so potentially powerful as analogues for congregational character. Within Christian "myths" the congregation can also discover clues for its own transformation.

Chapter 4. Preaching as Local Theology

1. Douglas John Hall, *Thinking the Faith: Christian Theology in a North American Context* (Minneapolis: Augsburg, 1989; paperback reprint, Fortress Press, 1992), 323–24.

2. See Robert Schreiter, *Constructing Local Theologies* (Maryknoll, N.Y.: Orbis, 1985), 22–38.

3. Barbara Brown Taylor, *The Preaching Life* (Boston: Cowley, 1993), 53–54.

4. Leander Keck, *The Bible in the Pulpit: The Renewal of Biblical Preaching* (Nashville: Abingdon, 1978), 105–07.

5. Hall, *Thinking the Faith*, 278.

6. Ibid., 280–81.

7. Ibid., 281.

8. David Buttrick, *Homiletic: Moves and Structures* (Philadelphia: Fortress Press, 1987), 18.

9. One of the constitutional questions addressed to all candidates for ministry in the Presbyterian Church (U.S.A.) is: "Do you sincerely receive and adopt the essential tenets of the Reformed faith as expressed in the confessions of our Church as authentic and reliable expositions of what Scripture leads us to believe and do, and will you be instructed and led by those confessions as you lead the people of God?" Presbyterian Church (USA) *Book of Order* (Louisville: Office of the General Assembly, 1994–95), G-14.0405b(3).

10. Justo L. Gonzalez and Catherine Gunsalus Gonzalez, *Liberation Preaching: The Pulpit and the Oppressed* (Nashville: Abingdon, 1980), 50.

11. Walter Brueggemann, "The Social Nature of the Biblical Text for Preaching" in *Preaching as a Social Act: Theology and Practice*, ed. Arthur Van Seters (Nashville: Abingdon, 1988), 130.

12. For example, one of the problems with subsequent interpretations of Barth's "theology of crisis" is that theologians have not always recognized (a) the highly contextual nature of Barth's own theology, and (b) the profound significance a radically different context makes for reinterpretation of that theology's meaning in our day. The world of Germany under the Third Reich and other contemporary "worlds" have sometimes been prematurely collapsed, precluding the development of a theology that is as genuinely contextual for our day as Barth's was for his.

See George Lindbeck, *The Nature of Doctrine: Religion and Theology in a Postliberal Age* (Philadelphia: Westminster, 1984), for a helpful discussion of the way in which the church can continue to be guided by the regulative principles at work in doctrinal formulations, rather than by their particular applications in historic situations.

13. Heinz Zahrnt, *The Question of God: Protestant Theology in the Twentieth Century*, trans. R. A. Wilson (New York: Harcourt, Brace & World, 1969), 118.

14. The move toward lectionary preaching actually began earlier—in 1969—when the Roman Catholic Church produced a revised series of readings for each Sunday of the liturgical year, as well as for weekdays, feast days, sacraments, and other occasions. Several Protestant denominations (Presbyterian, Episcopal, Lutheran, Disciples of Christ, and United Church of Christ) subsequently adapted it for their own use, and published differing versions of the Roman lectionary in their respective service books. It was, in part, the proliferation of lectionaries that led the Consultation on Common Texts to develop *The Common Lectionary* (New York: Church Hymnal Corporation, 1983), and its successor *The Revised Common Lectionary* (Nashville: Abingdon, 1992).

15. Although a psalm or canticle is also proposed for each Sunday, the framers of the lectionary meant it primarily to be used as a liturgical response to the Old Testament lesson.

16. David Buttrick cites this study in his article, "Preaching the Lectionary: Two Cheers and Some Questions," *Reformed Liturgy and Music* 27, no. 2 (Spring 1994): 80.

17. W. Alfred Tisdale Jr. preached this sermon at First Presbyterian Church, Cranbury, N.J., on April 23, 1995. The sermon, based on John 20:19-31, was titled "Thomas's Honest Question and Christ's Honest Answer."

18. Fred B. Craddock, *Preaching* (Nashville: Abingdon, 1985), 105–07.

19. Ibid., 106.

20. Elizabeth Achtemeier, *Preaching from the Old Testament* (Louisville: Westminster/John Knox, 1989), 54–55.

21. Peter Lampe gave this lecture, entitled "The Corinthian Eucharistic Dinner Party: Exegesis of a Cultural Context (I Cor. 11:17-34)," as his inaugural address at Union Theological Seminary in Richmond, Virginia, in February 1991. The lecture was subsequently published in *Affirmation* 4, no. 2 (Fall 1991): 1–15.

22. W. Sibley Towner, "Holistic Exegesis," *Affirmation* 2, no. 7 (December 1983): 43–50.

23. Critiques of sole reliance on the historical-critical method have been offered by scholars such as Hans Frei (*The Eclipse of Biblical Narrative* [New Haven: Yale University Press, 1980]), Brevard Childs (*Introduction to the Old Testament as Scripture* [Philadelphia: Fortress Press, 1979]), and James Barr ("Historical Reading and the Theological Interpretation of Scripture," in *The Scope and Authority of the Bible* [Philadelphia: Westminister, 1981], 30–51).

24. Towner, "Holistic Exegesis," 49.

25. Ibid., 47.

26. Ibid., 47–48.

27. James F. Hopewell, *Congregation: Stories and Structures* (Philadelphia: Fortress Press, 1987), 10–11.

28. This sermon was preached by Thomas D. Hay at the Wallace Presbyterian Church, Wallace, N.C., on August 19, 1990.

29. Deborah Lauderbach preached this sermon, titled "Family is Whom You Know," at Three Chopt Presbyterian Church in Richmond, Virginia, in February 1993.

30. Tex Sample, *U.S. Lifestyles and Mainline Churches: A Key to Reaching People in the 90's* (Louisville: Westminster/John Knox, 1990), 74–75.

31. Ibid., 76.

32. See Walter Brueggemann, *The Prophetic Imagination* (Philadelphia: Fortress Press, 1978).

32. Allan Boesak, "The Reuben Option," in *Walking on Thorns: The Call to Christian Obedience* (Geneva: World Council of Churches, 1984), 38.

33. Ibid., 41.

34. Walter Brueggemann, "The Social Nature of the Biblical Text for Preaching," in *Preaching as a Social Act*, ed. Arthur Van Seters, 143.

35. Dr. Albert Curry Winn, then pastor of Second Presbyterian Church, Richmond, Virginia, preached this sermon titled "The Magic Bow" on July 1, 1979.

Chapter 5. Preaching as Folk Art

1. Elizabeth Achtemeier, *Preaching as Theology and Art* (Nashville: Abingdon, 1984), 52.

2. Charles L. Rice, *The Embodied Word: Preaching as Art and Liturgy* (Minneapolis: Fortress Press, 1991), 95–100.

3. Fred B. Craddock, *Preaching* (Nashville: Abingdon, 1985), 79.

4. Paul Scott Wilson, *Imagination of the Heart: New Understandings in Preaching* (Nashville: Abingdon, 1988), 41–42.

5. Clarence Jordan, *The Cotton Patch Version of Matthew and John* (New York: Association Press, 1970), 18.

6. Barbara Brown Taylor, *The Preaching Life* (Boston: Cowley, 1993), 49.

7. Pat Lawrence Shafer, pastor of a small but rapidly growing congregation in New York State, prepared and preached a sermon using this image during a "Women's Ways of Preaching" continuing education event at Princeton Theological Seminary in January 1995. Her text was Luke 5:1-11.

8. Elizabeth Achtemeier uses this image from Zech. 8:1-8 in her sermon "Of Children and Streets and the Kingdom," in *A Chorus of Witnesses: Model Sermons for Today's Preacher*, Thomas G. Long and Cornelius Plantinga, Jr., eds. (Grand Rapids, Mich.: Wm. B. Eerdmans, 1994), 62–70.

9. Anna Carter Florence uses this image in her sermon "At the River's Edge," in *A Chorus of Witnesses*, ed. Long and Plantinga, 171–78.

10. Karen Pidcock-Lester used this image in a sermon entitled "Ordinary Time" that was preached at Second Presbyterian Church, Richmond, Virginia in 1990.

11. Joseph B. Martin IV preached this sermon during a "Congregational Context for Preaching" course at Union Theological Seminary in Virginia in 1992. The sermon, entitled "Andrew's Guide to Fishing," was prepared for a Disciples of Christ congregation in Richmond where he served as a student intern.

12. Amy Scott Vaughn, Associate Pastor for Christian Education and Youth at the First Presbyterian Church of Cranbury, New Jersey, used this image in a sermon she preached entitled "Where You Would Rather Not Go" on April 30, 1995. The biblical text for her sermon was John 21:15-19.

13. When I was a student at Union Theological Seminary in Virginia in the 1970s, Dr. Balmer Kelly, Professor of New Testament, preached a sermon in the seminary chapel in which he likened the woman's anointing of Jesus' feet to the gift of handmade wax flowers a widow had presented to the seminary around the turn of the century. He actually brought the faded flower arrangement (housed in the seminary archives) with him to chapel as a visual symbol of his proclamation.

14. Lydia and John are not their real names.

15. A psalm, for example, suggests—by its very form—that it should be preached differently than either a portion of a theological argument from Romans, or an encoded apocalyptic text from Revelation. For two excellent resources in this area, see David L. Bartlett, *The Shape of Scriptural Authority* (Philadelphia: Fortress Press, 1983), and Thomas G. Long, *Preaching and the Literary Forms of the Bible* (Philadelphia: Fortress Press, 1989).

16. Fred B. Craddock argued in *As One Without Authority: Essays on Inductive Preaching* (Enid, Okla.: Phillips University Press, 1974) that sermons should be shaped inductively because people (universally) live and come to understanding in their everyday lives by induction, not deduction. "Everyone lives inductively, not deductively," 63.

More recently David Buttrick (*Homiletic: Moves and Structures*, [Philadelphia: Fortress Press, 1987]) has argued that human beings universally participate in a shared structure of "human consciousness" that should be a primary consideration in the designing of sermon movement and structure.

17. Mary Field Belenky, et al., *Women's Ways of Knowing: The Development of Self, Voice, and Mind* (New York: Basic Books, 1986).

18. Robert J. Schreiter, *Constructing Local Theologies* (Maryknoll, N.Y.: Orbis, 1985), 75–94.

Bibliography

Abbey, Merrill. *Communication in Pulpit and Parish.* Philadelphia: Westminister Press, 1973.

Achtemeier, Elizabeth. "Of Children and Streets and the Kingdom." In *A Chorus of Witnesses: Model Sermons for Today's Preacher,* edited by Thomas G. Long and Cornelius Plantinga, Jr. 62–70. Grand Rapids, Mich.: Wm. B. Eerdmans, 1994.

————. *Preaching as Theology and Art.* Nashville: Abingdon Press, 1984.

————. *Preaching from the Old Testament.* Louisville: Westminister/ John Knox Press, 1989.

Augustine, St. *The First Catechetical Instruction* (*De Catechizondis Rudibus*). No. 2 in *Ancient Christian Writers.* Translated and annotated by Joseph P. Christopher. Westminister, Md.: Newman Bookshop, 1946.

————. *On Christian Doctrine.* Translated by D. W. Robertson, Jr. Indianapolis: Bobbs-Merrill Educational Publishing, 1958.

Barr, James. "Historical Reading and the Theological Interpretation of Scripture." In *The Scope and Authority of the Bible.* 30–51. Philadelphia: Westminster Press, 1981.

Barth, Karl. *The Preaching of the Gospel.* Translated by B. E. Hooke. Philadelphia: Westminister Press, 1987.

————. *The Word of God and the Word of Man.* New York: Harper & Row, 1957.

Bartlett, David L. *The Shape of Scriptural Authority.* Philadelphia: Fortress Press, 1983.

Battles, Ford Lewis. "God Was Accommodating Himself to Human Capacity." In *Readings in Calvin's Theology,* edited by Donald J. McKim. 21–42. Grand Rapids, Mich.: Baker Books, 1984.

Belenky, Mary Field, Blythe McVicker Clinchy, Nancy Rule Goldberger, Jill Mattuck Tarule. *Women's Ways of Knowing: The Development of Self, Voice, and Mind.* New York: Basic Books, 1968.

Bellah, Robert N., Richard Madsen, William M. Sullivan, Ann Swidler, and Stephen M. Tipton. *Habits of the Heart: Individualism and Commitment in American Life*. Berkeley and Los Angeles: University of California Press, 1985.

Bevans, Stephen B. *Models of Contextual Theology*. Maryknoll, N.Y.: Orbis Books, 1992.

———. "Models of Contextual Theology." *Missiology: An International Review* 13, no. 2 (April 1985): 185–202.

Boesak, Allan. "The Reuben Option." In *Walking on Thorns: The Call to Christian Obedience*. Geneva: World Council of Churches, 1984.

Bowen, Murray. *Family Therapy in Clinical Practice*. New York: J. Aranson, 1978.

Brueggemann, Walter. *The Prophetic Imagination*. Philadelphia: Fortress Press, 1978.

———. "The Preacher, Text, and People." *Theology Today* 47 (October 1990): 237–47.

———. "The Social Nature of the Biblical Text for Preaching." In *Preaching as a Social Act: Theology and Practice*, edited by Arthur Van Seters. 127–65. Nashville: Abingdon Press, 1988.

Brunner, Emil. *Natural Theology: Comprising "Nature and Grace."* Translated by Peter Fraenkel. London: G. Bles, The Centenary Press, 1946.

Buttrick, David. *Homiletic: Moves and Structures*. Philadelphia: Fortress Press, 1987.

———. "Preaching the Lectionary: Two Cheers and Some Questions." *Reformed Liturgy and Music* 27, no. 2 (Spring 1994): 80.

Calvin, John. *Institutes of the Christian Religion*. The Library of Christian Classics, edited by John T. McNeill, translated by Ford Lewis Battles. Philadelphia: Westminister Press, 1960.

Capps, Donald. *Pastoral Counseling and Preaching: A Quest for an Integrated Ministry*. Philadelphia: Westminster Press, 1980.

Cardenal, Ernesto. *The Gospel in Solentiname*, Vols. 1–4. Translated by Donald D. Walsh. Maryknoll, N.Y.: Orbis Books, 1976, 1978, 1979, and 1982.

Carl, William J., III. *Preaching Christian Doctrine*. Philadelphia: Fortress Press, 1984.

Carroll, Jackson W., Carl S. Dudley, and William McKinney, eds. *Handbook for Congregational Studies*. Nashville: Abingdon Press, 1986.

Chapple, Eliot D., and Carleton Coon. *Principles of Anthropology.* New York: Holt, Rinehart & Winston, 1942.

Childs, Brevard. *Introduction to the Old Testament as Scripture.* Philadelphia: Fortress Press, 1979.

Clark, Linda J. "Hymn-Singing: The Congregation Making Faith." In *Carriers of Faith: Lessons from Congregational Studies,* edited by Carl S. Dudley, Jackson W. Carroll, and James P. Wind. Louisville: Westminister/John Knox Press, 1991.

Clifton, James. "Ethnography." In *Encyclopedia of Anthropology,* edited by David E. Hunter and Phillip Whitten. 148. New York: Harper & Row, 1976.

Consultation on Common Texts. *The Common Lectionary.* New York: The Church Hymnal Corporation, 1983.

———. *The Revised Common Lectionary.* Nashville: Abingdon Press, 1992.

Craddock, Fred B. *As One Without Authority: Essays on Inductive Preaching.* Enid, Okla.: Phillips University Press, 1974.

———. *Overhearing the Gospel.* Nashville: Abingdon Press, 1978.

———. *Preaching.* Nashville: Abingdon Press, 1985.

Douglas, Mary. *Natural Symbols: Explorations in Cosmology.* New York: Pantheon, 1982.

Dudley, Carl S., and James Hopewell. "Understanding and Activating Congregations," in *Building Effective Ministry: Theory and Practice in the Local Church,* edited by Carl S. Dudley. 246–56. San Francisco: Harper & Row, 1983.

Dudley, Carl S. and Sally A. Johnson. "Congregational Self-Images for Social Ministry." In *Carriers of Faith: Lessons from Congregational Studies,* edited by Carl S. Dudley, Jackson W. Carroll, and James P. Wind. 104–22. Louisville: Westminister/John Knox Press, 1991.

Dulles, Avery. *Models of Revelation.* Garden City, N.Y.: Image Books, 1985.

———. *Models of the Church.* Garden City, N.Y.: Image Books, 1978.

Fant, Clyde. *Bonhoeffer: Worldly Preaching.* Nashville: Thomas J. Nelson, 1975.

Florence, Anna Carter. "At the River's Edge." In *A Chorus of Witnesses: Model Sermons for Today's Preacher,* edited by Thomas G. Long and Cornelius Plantinga, Jr. Grand Rapids, Mich.: Wm. B. Eerdmans, 1994.

Frei, Hans. *The Eclipse of Biblical Narrative.* New Haven: Yale University Press, 1974.

Friedman, Edwin H. *Generation to Generation: Family Process in Church and Synagogue.* New York: Guilford Press, 1985.

Gadamer, Hans-Georg. *Truth and Method.* New York: Crossroad, 1984.

Geertz, Clifford. *The Interpretation of Cultures.* New York: Basic Books, 1973.

———. *Local Knowledge: Further Essays in Interpretive Anthropology.* New York: Basic Books, 1983.

Gerkin, Charles. *Widening the Horizons: Pastoral Responses to a Fragmented Society.* Philadelphia: Westminister Press, 1988.

Gonzalez, Justo L. and Catherine Gunsalus Gonzalez. *Liberation Preaching: The Pulpit and the Oppressed.* Nashville: Abingdon Press, 1980.

Green, Garrett. *Imagining God: Theology and the Religious Imagination.* San Francisco: Harper & Row, 1989.

Grierson, Denham. *Transforming a People of God.* Melbourne: The Joint Board of Christian Education of Australia and New Zealand, 1984.

Guthrie, Stewart. "Ritual." In *Encyclopedia of Anthropology*, edited by David E. Hunter and Phillip Whitten. 336–37. New York: Harper & Row, 1976.

Hall, Douglas John. *Thinking the Faith: Christian Theology in a North American Context.* Minneapolis: Augsburg, 1989; paperback reprint, Fortress Press, 1992.

Hamilton, Neill Q. "Friday Morning Comments on the Handbook." Correspondence with the editors of *Handbook for Congregational Studies*, eds. Jackson W. Carroll, Carl S. Dudley, & William McKinney. Nashville: Abingdon Press, 1986.

Harris, Marvin. *Cultural Anthropology.* New York: Harper & Row, 1983.

———. *Cultural Materialism: The Struggle for a Science of Culture.* New York: Random House, 1979.

———. *The Rise of Anthropological Theory: A History of Theories and Culture.* New York: Thomas Y. Crowell, 1968.

Hopewell, James F. *Congregation: Stories and Structures.* Edited by Barbara G. Wheeler. Philadelphia: Fortress Press, 1987.

Howe, Reuel. *Partners in Preaching: Clergy and Laity in Dialogue.* New York: The Seabury Press, 1967.

Hunter, David E., and Phillip Whitten, eds. *Encyclopedia of Anthropology.* New York: Harper & Row, 1976.

Hunter, Edwina. "The Preacher as a Social Being in the Community of Faith." In *Preaching as a Social Act: Theology and Practice*, edited by Arthur Van Seters. 95–125. Nashville: Abingdon Press, 1988.

Jackson, Edgar. *A Psychology for Preaching*. Great Neck, N.Y.: Channel Press, 1961.

Jordan, Clarence. *The Cotton Patch Version of Matthew and John*. New York: Association Press, 1970.

Keck, Leander. *The Bible in the Pulpit: The Renewal of Biblical Preaching*. Nashville: Abingdon Press, 1978.

Kelsey, David H. *The Uses of Scripture in Recent Theology*. Philadelphia: Fortress Press, 1975.

Kluckhohn, Clyde, and Henry Murray. *Personality in Nature, Society, and Culture*. New York: Alfred A. Knopf, 1948.

Kluckhohn, Clyde, et al. "Values and Value-Orientations in the Theory of Action: An Exploration in Definition and Classification." In *Toward a General Theory of Action*, edited by Talcott Parsons and Edward A. Shils. 388–433. Cambridge: Harvard University Press, 1951.

Kluckhohn, Florence Rockwood, and Fred L. Strodtbeck. *Variations in Value Orientations*. Evanston, Ill. and Elmsford, N.Y.: Row, Peterson & Co., 1961.

Kraft, Charles H. *Christianity in Culture: A Study in Dynamic Biblical Theologizing in Cross-Cultural Perspective*. Maryknoll, N.Y.: Orbis Books, 1984.

Lampe, Peter. "The Corinthian Eucharistic Dinner Party: Exegesis of a Cultural Context (I Cor. 11:17-34)." In *Affirmation* 4, no. 2 (Fall 1991): 1–15.

Leith, John H. *Introduction to the Reformed Tradition*. Atlanta: John Knox Press, 1977.

———. "Reformed Preaching Today." *Princeton Seminary Bulletin* 10, no. 3 (1989): 224–57.

Lindbeck, George. *The Nature of Doctrine: Religion and Theology in a Postliberal Age*. Philadelphia: Westminister Press, 1984.

Long, Thomas G. *Preaching and the Literary Forms of the Bible*. Philadelphia: Fortress Press, 1989.

———. *The Witness of Preaching*. Louisville: Westminister/John Knox Press, 1989.

Luzbetak, Louis. "Signs of Progress in Contextual Methodology." *Verbum svd* 22 (1981): 39–57.

Malinowski, Bronislaw. *Argonauts of the Western Pacific.* New York: Dutton, 1961.

Marty, Martin E. *A Nation of Believers.* Chicago: University of Chicago Press, 1976.

McFague, Sallie. *Metaphorical Theology: Models of God in Religious Language.* Philadelphia: Fortress Press, 1982.

———. *Models of God: Theology for an Ecological, Nuclear Age.* Philadelphia: Fortress Press, 1987.

Migliore, Daniel L. *Faith Seeking Understanding.* Grand Rapids, Mich.: Wm. B. Eerdmans, 1991.

Mitchell, Henry H. *The Recovery of Preaching.* San Francisco: Harper & Row, 1977.

———. *Black Preaching.* San Franscisco: Harper & Row, 1979.

Nelson, C. Ellis. *Congregations: Their Power to Form and Transform.* Atlanta: John Knox Press, 1988.

———. *Where Faith Begins.* Richmond: John Knox Press, 1967.

Nelson, Hart M., and Mary Ann Maguire. "The Two Worlds of Clergy and Congregation: Dilemma for Mainline Denominations." *Sociological Analysis* (Spring 1980).

Nichols, J. Randall. *Building the Word: The Dynamics of Communication and Preaching.* San Francisco: Harper & Row, 1980.

———. *The Restoring Word: Preaching as Pastoral Communication.* San Francisco: Harper & Row, 1987.

Niebuhr, H. Richard. *Christ and Culture.* New York: Harper & Row, 1951.

———. *The Meaning of Revelation.* New York: Macmillan, 1941.

———. *The Social Sources of Denominationalism.* New York: Henry Holt, 1929.

Oswald, Roy M. *Crossing the Boundary between Seminary and Parish.* Washington, D.C.: The Alban Institute, 1979.

Pitt-Watson, Ian. *A Kind of Folly: Toward a Practical Theology of Preaching.* Edinburgh: St. Andrew, 1976.

Porter, Richard E., and Larry A. Samovar. "Approaching Intercultural Communication." In *Intercultural Communication: A Reader,* 5th ed. Belmont, Calif.: Wadsworth, 1988.

Presbyterian Church (USA). *Book of Order* (1994–1995). Louisville: Office of the General Assembly.

Redfield, Robert. *The Primitive World and Its Transformations.* Ithaca, N.Y.: Cornell University Press, 1953.

Rice, Charles L. *The Embodied Word: Preaching as Art and Liturgy.* Minneapolis: Fortress Press, 1991.

Roof, Wade Clark. *Community and Commitment: Religious Plausibility in a Liberal Protestant Church.* New York: Elsevier, 1978.

Roof, Wade Clark, and William McKinney. *American Mainline Religion: Its Changing Shape and Future.* New Brunswick: Rutgers University Press, 1987.

Roozen, David A., William McKinney, and Jackson W. Carroll. *Varieties of Religious Presence: Mission in Public Life.* New York: Pilgrim Press, 1984.

Ruben, Brent D. "Human Communication and Cross-Cultural Effectiveness." In *Intercultural Communication: A Reader,* rev. ed., edited by Richard E. Porter and Larry A. Samovar. 338–46. New Brunswick: Transaction Books, 1988.

Sample, Tex. *U. S. Lifestyles and Mainline Churches: A Key to Reaching People in the 90's.* Louisville: Westminister/John Knox Press, 1990.

Sarbaugh, L. E. *Intercultural Communication.* rev. ed. New Brunswick: Transaction Books, 1988.

Schreiter, Robert J. *Constructing Local Theologies.* Maryknoll, N.Y.: Orbis Books, 1985.

Stackhouse, Max. "Contextualization, Contextuality, and Contextualism." In *One Faith, Many Cultures: Inculturation, Indigenization, and Contextualization,* edited by Ruy O. Costa. 3–13. Maryknoll, N.Y.: Orbis Books, 1988.

Steimle, Edmund A., Morris J. Niedenthal, and Charles L. Rice, eds. *Preaching the Story.* Philadelphia: Fortress Press, 1980.

Stokes, Allison, and David A. Roozen. "The Unfolding Story of Congregational Studies." In *Carriers of Faith: Lessons from Congregational Studies,* edited by Carl S. Dudley, Jackson W. Carroll, and James P. Wind. 183–92. Louisville: Westminister/John Knox Press, 1991.

Taylor, Barbara Brown. *The Preaching Life.* Boston: Cowley Publications, 1993.

Taylor, Mark Kline. *Beyond Explanation: Religious Dimensions in Cultural Anthropology.* Macon, Ga.: Mercer University Press, 1986.

Thomas, M. M. "An Irrelevant Profession?" *Student World* (Fourth Quarter 1950): no pagination.

————. *Toward a Theology of Contemporary Ecumenism: A Collection of Addresses to Ecumenical Gatherings (1947–1975)*. Madras, India: The Christian Literature Society, 1978.

Tillich, Paul. *Theology of Culture*. Edited by Robert C. Kimball. New York: Oxford University Press, 1959.

Towner, W. Sibley. "Holistic Exegesis." *Affirmation* 2, no. 7 (December 1983): 43–50.

Troeger, Thomas H. *Borrowed Light: Hymn Texts, Prayers, Poems*. New York: Oxford University Press, 1994.

Turner, Victor. *Dramas, Fields, and Metaphors*. Ithaca, N.Y.: Cornell University Press, 1974.

Turner, Victor, and Edith Turner. *Image and Pilgrimage in Christian Culture: Anthropological Perspectives*. New York: Columbia University Press, 1978.

Van Seters, Arthur, ed. *Preaching as a Social Act: Theology and Practice*. Nashville: Abingdon Press, 1988.

Walrath, Douglas A. "Types of Small Congregations and Their Implications for Planning." In *Small Churches Are Beautiful*, edited by Jackson W. Carroll. 33–61. San Francisco: Harper & Row, 1977.

Wardlaw, Don M. "Preaching as the Interface of Two Social Worlds: The Congregation as Corporate Agent in the Act of Preaching." In *Preaching as a Social Act: Theology and Practice*, edited by Arthur Van Seters. 55–93. Nashville: Abingdon Press, 1988.

————. ed. *Preaching Biblically*. Philadelphia: Westminister Press, 1983.

Welsh, Clement. *Preaching in a New Key: Studies in the Psychology of Thinking and Listening*. Philadelphia: United Church Press, 1974.

Wilson, Paul Scott. *Imagination of the Heart: New Understandings in Preaching*. Nashville: Abingdon Press, 1988.

Wind, James. *Places of Worship: Exploring Their History*. Edited by David E. Kyvig and Myron A. Marty. The Nearby History Series, no. 4. Nashville: American Association for State and Local History, 1990.

Wood, Charles M. *The Formation of Christian Understanding: An Essay in Theological Hermeneutics*. Philadelphia: Westminister Press, 1981.

Zahrnt, Heinz. *The Question of God: Protestant Theology in the Twentieth Century*. Translated by R. A. Wilson. New York: Harcourt, Brace & World, 1969.

Index

167

DATE DUE